FOOTBALL *Widows* HANDBOOK

An Illustrated Guide to the Game of Professional Football

BY
PATRICIA MOONEY GONZALEZ

ILLUSTRATED BY YURI PASS

COVE PRESS

Cove Press is an imprint of U.S. Games Systems, Inc.
Stamford, CT 06902 USA

Library of Congress Number: 95-070425

ISBN 1-57281-007-6

10 9 8 7 6 5 4 3 2 1

Printed in USA

COVE PRESS
An imprint of U.S. Games Systems, Inc.
179 Ludlow Street
Stamford, CT 06902 USA

This book is dedicated to my father, Frank Mooney, who instilled in me a love for football; and to my late mother, Jeanne Mooney, who for many years graciously scheduled Sunday dinner around the playing schedule of the New York Giants.

ACKNOWLEDGMENTS

I would like to extend heartfelt thanks to the following individuals for their support and assistance as I was writing this book. I greatly appreciate all of their efforts.

To "Berry" for being "Berry." To my sisters Kathy Mooney and Mary Beth Mooney Fine, my brother-in-law Randy Fine, our "adopted sister" Debra Francescott, and more recently, our stepmother Joan Fenn Mooney, for making family gatherings on Sunday afternoons during football season something to look forward to.

To Carol Wickert Perry for her encouragement and support; to the "guinea pigs" in my football classes for making me aware of the many preconceived notions about the game of football.

To Gail Samuelson, Dr. Camille Fareri, Ann Mattei, and Dr. Russell Kratz for lending their critical eyes to this book and for offering insightful suggestions.

To my colleagues Grant L. Miller and Tom Walters for providing me with up-to-date information on the game, NFL players, rules, all sorts of "football numbers" and interesting trivia.

To Jack Reader, Jay Monahan and Reggie Roberts of the National Football League for patiently answering all my questions and clarifying some of the more confusing aspects of the game.

To Mr. Wellington Mara, the classy owner of the New York Giants, for providing me with interesting background information.

Most of all, I would like to thank Diane Diaz for all her invaluable assistance in the typing of this book. Without her patience, cooperation and hard work during all the hours of writing, rewriting and more rewriting, this book would have never become a reality. Diane, you have no idea what a real treasure you are! Muchas Gracias!

TABLE OF CONTENTS

PROLOGUE

> "'Twas the morn before football,
> Before the first punt or hike
> Not a creature was stirring,
> Not even our Mike.
>
> His things were all placed
> By the TV with care,
> In hopes that the NFL
> Soon would be there.
>
> When from out of his clock,
> There arose such a ringing
> That our Motley leapt up
> And to his den went a-winging.
>
> He aimed his remote,
> And gave it a click.
> And smiled as the season's
> First pigskin was kicked. (And there's the kickoff!)
>
> Upon hearing these words,
> Mabel's heart it did sadden.
> For she knew she faced
> Six whole months of John Madden."

Source: "Motley's Crew," by Ben Templeton and Tom Forman. New York Daily News, September, 1993.

The above scenario is played out all over America every September. But it wasn't until I began offering Football Basics workshops that I began to fully realize just how many people, particularly women, actually dread the yearly onset of the professional football season. I've been an avid football fan since I was a young child; therefore it had never occurred to me that there were many people out there who just didn't understand football, but may want to learn the game.

As each summer draws to a close and the pre-season games begin, suffering souls like Mabel in the poem experience another season of anger, frustration, and boredom at the thought of having to endure another six months of football. They may want to understand the basics of the game, but have never had the opportunity to learn. Since I had learned "Football as a Second Language" as a young child, I found it difficult to empathize with these folks. Having been fortunate enough to never have felt excluded at sporting events, for a long time I've been able to participate in sports-related discussions without fear, ridicule or embarrassment. In short, it was hard for me to comprehend the feelings of Mabel and other people like her.

That is—until Trinidad.

It was during a three-week visit to Trinidad in the British West Indies in February of 1993 that I began to empathize with the long-suffering football novices in the United States. It was then and only then that I slowly began to understand what these individuals had been telling me all along about their feelings of exclusion, especially as it related to the world of sports. How did I finally begin to see the light? Cricket!

Trinidadians, like most West Indians, are fanatical about cricket, an outdoor game played between two teams of eleven players each, with wickets, bat and ball. What I knew about cricket could fit in a pig's ear with plenty of storage room left over. I would see Trinidadians of all ages, after rising out of a sound sleep at 3 o'clock in the morning, sit glued for hours in front of their television sets to watch their West Indies team play against Pakistan, England, Australia, and South Africa. News of the progress of the West Indies team constantly filled the airwaves, and Trinidadians were never far from their radios or TV's when satellites beamed in the games.

How did I, an avid sports fan, react to all this cricket fanaticism? Was I able to have all my questions answered and have the game explained to me while a group of fans was watching TV? You've got to be kidding! I would stare blankly at the television screen and try to figure out the basics of the game by myself, but to no avail (I was reminded on several occasions that cricketers play "matches," not "games"). The Trinidadians would try to help by telling me, "It's kind of like your American baseball." The only similarity I could draw between cricket and baseball without anyone actually taking the time to explain the game was that both sports use a ball and bat.

I even went to watch a local cricket game – pardon me, match (old habits are so hard to break!) – but that proved to be useless. Hearing and being surrounded by lively discussions about "wicket keepers," "silly mid-ons," "silly mid-offs," "leg breaks," "byes," "slips," "maiden overs," "yorkers," and my personal favorite, "googlies," made me think at times that I had been mysteriously transported to another planet and was totally unable to communicate in "cricket," the planet's host language.

Since I hold the firm belief that people tend to learn best when new material is presented to them in a variety of formats, I had a brilliant idea. Since I couldn't learn the game by just watching television, and since I didn't have any kind of a cricket background to ask any intelligent questions, I decided that I would learn about cricket on my own – by reading about it.

This stroke of creative genius made perfect sense to me at the time. However, as I trudged through Trinidadian bookstore after bookstore in Port of Spain, San Fernando, and even Saint Augustine where the University of the West Indies (UWI) is located, it became increasingly apparent that I would not be successful in finding any material which would meet my needs. Although there was an abundance of cricket materials available, they tended to be of biographical, historical, and statistical content, rather than of an instructional nature. I had exhausted my last alternative and continued throughout the remainder of my stay in Trinidad to watch cricket in frustration, wanting, but not being able, to follow any of the matches' action. I began to ask myself, "Pat, you are now feeling frustrated, excluded, angry, disinterested and absolutely bored to tears. Have you ever heard any similar complaints about sports expressed to you before?"

As I sat watching my final cricket match on television in Trinidad, I began to really understand the feelings of those Americans, who for whatever reason traditionally have not had a viable vehicle for learning professional football and who suffer through what seems to them to be endlessly long football seasons year after year. It was right then and there that I decided to write this book.

I trust that upon finishing the *Football Widows Handbook* you will come away armed with a basic knowledge of professional football and can then apply the information to best meet your particular needs. If this book can help to ease some of your feelings of boredom, exclusion, or frustration (similar to my cricket experience), or maybe make you a fan of the game, I will consider its writing to have been a worthwhile endeavor.

Patricia Mooney Gonzalez, Ph.D.
1995

PURPOSE OF THE BOOK

The purpose of this book is to provide you with a brief explanation of the fundamentals of professional football as it is played in the National Football League. Most of the material currently available on football assumes that the reader has a basic knowledge of the game; books usually take the form of autobiographies, team histories, strength and conditioning guides, and coaching manuals. These materials often contain large amounts of unexplained football terminology, leaving the football novice still frustrated and lacking a means to learn the game on his or her own.

Football Widows Handbook introduces you to professional football, beginning with the game's basic elements. It is intended for anyone who wants to enhance their knowledge about one of the most popular spectator sports in the United States. The book lends itself nicely to being a quick reference guide that you can carry anywhere.

This guide includes step-by-step discussions of players, formations, scoring, penalties, and other topics presented in a hierarchical fashion, much like a textbook in which each chapter builds upon the information learned in the previous ones. Although it is intended as a guide to the basics, the book includes a list of recommended readings so that you can investigate more complex aspects of the game on your own, should you choose to do so.

Football Widows Handbook

This book is organized according to certain instructional principles so that you can learn at your own pace and can review difficult or confusing material when necessary. Although you are all learning or reviewing the game of football for a variety of reasons and come from diverse backgrounds, the book is organized to meet your unique needs.

We begin with a short questionnaire entitled, *How Much Do You Know Already?* which serves as a pre-test of sorts for you. It lets you know what you know and what you don't know about professional football. By taking this pre-test, you will be better able to select the particular chapters that best meet your needs.

I believe that you can obtain the most benefit from this book by doing the following:

- Take the *How Much Do You Know Already?* pre-test. Record your answers and save the sheet for future reference. Review your answer sheet and find out which chapters contain the information with which you had the most difficulty. Some beginners may know very little about football and may need to read every chapter. Others may find that they need a refresher on penalties (Chapter 10) or statistics (Chapter 12), and can then concentrate on those chapters.

- Read each chapter carefully and pay particular attention to the accompanying drawings and diagrams. They will help you understand some of the basic concepts presented in the text. In addition, keep an eye out for the words that are printed in bold type; this indicates the importance of particular football vocabulary words and expressions.

- At the end of each chapter, read the *Checklist: Things to Remember* and *Terms to Know*, which summarize the important points of the chapter. Try to familiarize yourself with the terms and concepts before you move on to the next chapter.

- After you have read the book, you should complete the questionnaire entitled, *How Much Do You Know Now?* located at the end of the book. This questionnaire has a dual purpose: it documents all the progress you've made and it identifies those areas which you may still need to review. Compare your answers from *How Much Do You Know Now?* to your answers from *How Much Do Know Already?* Trust me, you'll be amazed at how much you've learned!

- Take the *Football Scenarios Quiz* that appears in Appendix A. This quiz presents exercises in which you must apply your newly acquired or refresher information to actual football situations. You are the coach and are asked to make decisions similar to those that every coach makes during a football game. If you can make it through this set of exercises successfully, you have done a good job in familiarizing yourself with the basics of professional football.

Good luck to each and every one of you! I know your reasons for wanting to learn this game are undoubtedly as varied as those of the people who have attended my football workshops: a 73-year old widow who used televised football games on Sunday afternoons as a companion; mothers who wanted to know more about the action on the field during their sons' Pop Warner, high school, and college football games; a criminal lawyer who wanted to understand football analogies and terms commonly used by his law partners; women of all ages and backgrounds who were surrounded by all sorts of professional football fanatics in their lives; and a female college dean who was struggling with "The Green Ceiling" in business and wanted to communicate more effectively with her male coworkers in what has traditionally been considered to be the language of men: sports talk.

Although your interest, motivation and experience may vary a great deal, I hope you all achieve your personal goals in learning about football, and developing or enhancing your enjoyment of this game. Who knows? Some of you may even become real football fans, may begin to follow the progress of a particular team, or may even come to look forward to Sunday afternoons and Monday nights during football season!

HOW MUCH DO YOU KNOW ALREADY?

(answers on p. xvi)

1. What is the NFL?_____

2. How many players can a football team have on the field at one time? _____

3. What is the offense?_____

4. Name the five ways a team can score points.
   a. _____
   b. _____
   c. _____
   d. _____
   e. _____

5. What are the dimensions of a football field?

   _____

6. How are inbound lines/hashmarks used? _____

   _____

7. What is the major responsibility of the referee?

   _____

8. Identify the jersey numbers assigned to running backs. _____

9. What is a down marker?_____

   _____

10. What is the shotgun formation? _____

_____

11. Name two of the player positions that make up
    the offensive line.
    a. _____
    b. _____

12 What is the front four? _____

_____

13. What does a holder do? _____

_____

14. What is sudden death? _____

_____

15. What is decided during a coin toss? _____

_____

16. On what yard line do kickoffs originate? _____

17. Where are the "trenches" or the "pits"? _____

_____

18. How many minutes of playing time are there in a
    regulation professional football game? _____

_____

19. What is the two-minute warning? _____

_____

20. How many time outs per half is each team allowed? _____

21. What is the down and distance rule?_____
_____

22. What happens during a bootleg play?_____
_____

23. What is the purpose of the pocket?_____
_____

24. What is a bomb? _____

25. What does the first digit in an alignment refer to?
_____

23. What is a dime defense? _____
_____

24. What is a blitz?_____
_____

25. Name two types of pass defense.
    a. _____
    b. _____

26. Name two of the six special team units on a football team.
    a. _____
    b. _____

27. How far does an onside kick have to travel to be legal? _____

28. What is hang time? _____

29. What is a fair catch? _____

30. On what yard line is the ball placed for an extra point attempt? _____

31. How many members make up an officiating crew?

_____

32. Who is the chief official? _____

33. How does an official signal that a touchdown, field goal, or extra point has been scored?

_____

37. What is a penalty marker? _____

_____

38. What are offsetting penalties? _____

_____

39. What does roughing the kicker mean? _____

_____

40. What is the amount of penalty yardage assessed for unsportsmanlike conduct? _____

ANSWERS

LIST OF DIAGRAMS, DRAWINGS AND FIGURES

CHAPTER 1
OVERVIEW OF THE GAME

"I never see much kicking going on; I wonder why they call this game football." - Carol Perry (1987)

Football has evolved to refer to any of several team games including American football, English rugby, association football (soccer), touch football, Australian football, and Canadian football. But in the United States, **football** means the American game as played by high school, college, and professional teams. Modern American football is played chiefly in the United States, but in recent years it has become increasingly popular in Japan, Europe, Latin America, and other parts of the world. Although the game is played in many ways and at different levels (e.g., touch football, flag football, tackle football, youth league, high school football, and college football), for purposes of this book we will confine our discussion to professional football as it is played in the **National Football League (NFL)**.

What is football?

Football is a game played by two teams of 11 players each, played with an oval-shaped leather ball on a rectangular field having a Y-shaped goal post and a 10-yard **end zone** at either end. The object of the game is to score more points than the opponent by advancing the ball past the opponent's goal line. Players advance the ball by running or passing maneuvers called **plays** that move the ball up and down the field. Between plays, the players rest and then decide on strategies for their next play. Even though the game is called football, kicking plays a relatively minor role other than in **kickoffs, field goals** and **conversions (extra points)**.

During the course of a game, possession of the football switches back and forth between the two opposing teams. Professional football uses a two-platoon system that allows for substitutions, so that the same players are not on the field all the time. Each team has players that make up an **offensive unit**, which plays when its team has the ball. Other players make up a **defensive unit**, which plays when the opposing team has the ball. The offense tries to advance the ball down the field; if it can move the ball across its opponent's goal line or can kick the ball over its opponent's goal post, it scores points. The defensive unit tries to stop the progress of the offense and prevent it from scoring.

The game of football involves a rhythm, with all the action starting and stopping in spurts called **plays**. All important aspects of the game occur during plays. It is during plays that the team with the ball can advance it, score points, get pushed backward or lose it to the other team.

In addition to offensive and defensive units, a professional football team has **special teams**. These are the units that go on the field for kicking situations (kickoffs, field goals, punts, and extra points). Some players may be members of the offense only, the defense only, or special teams only, while others may play on several teams during a game. Team members may also play on more than one special team.

Scoring	A team can score points in five different ways:
	a. **Touchdown** (6 points)
	b. **Field goal** (3 points)
	c. **Safety** (2 points)
	d. **Extra Point** (1 point) Also called a point-after-touchdown (PAT) or 1-point conversion
	e. **Conversion** (2 points)
Time Periods	A football game is divided into four 15-minute **periods** or **quarters.** Although the actual playing time is only 60 minutes, a game takes much more time than that because the clock is stopped whenever play is suspended. There is also a 12-minute intermission called **halftime** between the second and third quarters of the game.
Officials	A football game is supervised by a seven-member squad of officials which makes sure that the game is played according to the rules. Each official has particular duties, but any one of the officials may call a violation. When a player breaks a rule, his team is assessed a **penalty** for the infraction. An official signals the violation by blowing his whistle and throwing a yellow cloth called a **penalty marker** in the air. The chief official, called the **referee**, signals what rule has been violated and assesses a penalty against the team guilty of the violation.
Organization	The National Football League (NFL) currently consists of 30 teams, each representing a city or region in the United States. The teams are divided

into two conferences, the **National Football Conference (NFC)** and the **American Football Conference (AFC)**, each with 15 teams. Each conference consists of three divisions: **Eastern, Central** and **Western**.

National Football League

AFC East	AFC Central	AFC West
Buffalo Bills	Cincinnati Bengals	Denver Broncos
Indianapolis Colts	Cleveland Browns	Kansas City Chiefs
Miami Dolphins	Houston Oilers	Oakland Raiders
New England Patriots	Jacksonville Jaguars	San Diego Chargers
New York Jets	Pittsburgh Steelers	Seattle Seahawks

NFC East	NFC Central	NFC West
Arizona Cardinals	Chicago Bears	Atlanta Falcons
Dallas Cowboys	Detroit Lions	Carolina Panthers
New York Giants	Green Bay Packers	New Orleans Saints
Philadelphia Eagles	Minnesota Vikings	St. Louis Rams
Washington Redskins	Tampa Bay Buccaneers	San Francisco 49ers

Note: The National Football League went through several changes in 1995-96. The first expansion since 1976 adds two new teams to the League: The Carolina Panthers, based in Charlotte, North Carolina; and the Jacksonville Jaguars, which makes its home in Jacksonville, Florida. In addition, the Los Angeles Rams moved to St. Louis, and the Los Angeles Raiders (formerly the Oakland Raiders) moved back to Oakland.

1.1 NFL TEAMS

Football Schedule

The six month NFL playing schedule is divided into three sections: pre-season, regular season and playoffs. NFL players report to training camp every July to prepare for the upcoming season. During camp sessions, players compete for slots on the roster; it is at this time that the coaching staff decides which players will make the team and which ones will be **"cut."** In August, to further prepare for the regular season, the teams play at least four **pre-season** or **exhibition** games, which do not count in the league standings or in the record books.

The NFL season officially begins with the playing of the **Hall of Fame Game** at the **Professional Football Hall of Fame** in Canton, Ohio. This game is a match-up between an AFC team and an NFC team selected at random and is usually played on the last Saturday in July. During this same Hall of Fame weekend, a ceremony is held in which a select group of retired NFL players are inducted into the Professional Football Hall of Fame.

In September, the NFL regular season schedule begins. Each team plays all of the other teams in its division twice: once home and once away. The remainder of the schedule is determined by a formula that considers the team's Won-Lost-Tied record from the previous year. Each team plays 16 games and receives one **bye** or off week.

After the regular season schedule is completed in late December or early January, qualifying teams advance to three rounds of post-season play called **playoffs,** which culminate in the **Super Bowl** game in late January. The Super Bowl game is an annual contest between the NFC and AFC champions to win the coveted Vince Lombardi Trophy, and has a worldwide television viewing audience of hundreds of millions of people.

The NFL season officially ends with the playing of the **Pro Bowl** game, the game held the week after the Super Bowl that puts all-stars from each conference against one another. These all-star players are chosen by NFL coaches and other NFL players.

In April of each year, NFL teams obtain college football players in a selection system known as the **draft.**

☑ CHAPTER 1 CHECKLIST
THINGS TO REMEMBER

- National Football League (NFL) – 30 teams – AFC and NFC
- Scoring: touchdown (6 points)
  field goal (3 points)
  safety (2 points)
  extra point (1 point)
  conversion (2 points)
- 60 minutes of playing time – four periods of 15 minutes each
- Seven officials – Chief official is the referee
- NFL schedule runs from August through January

TERMS TO KNOW

defense	offense	special team
draft	penalty marker	Super Bowl
halftime	pre-season game	

 EXTRA POINTS: DID YOU KNOW?

- According to **The 1995 Information Please Sports Almanac**, eight NFL teams have never appeared in the Super Bowl game: Cleveland Browns, Houston Oilers, Atlanta Falcons, Detroit Lions, Arizona Cardinals, New Orleans Saints, Seattle Seahawks, and Tampa Bay Buccaneers.

- The NFL had the longest off-season (the length of time between the end of one season and the beginning of another) among all of the major sports during 1993-94. According to USA Today research (1994), there were 161 days between the Super Bowl game and the first day of pro-football training camp. Other major league sports had shorter off-seasons: the National Basketball Association (NBA) had 106 days off, major league baseball players had 117 days to prepare, and the National Hockey League (NHL) were off the skating rink for only 81 days.

- The NFL instituted the 2-point conversion scoring rule in 1994, marking the first scoring rule change in 75 years.

CHAPTER 2

WHAT TO LOOK FOR

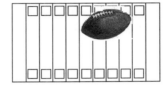

"Why do these big football players have such little rear ends?"
-Jeanne Mooney (1971)

The students in my Football Basics classes have said that a useful element of my instruction involves the identification of common items and terms that come up in actual game situations. They felt that once I helped them train their eyes and ears to focus on particular aspects of the game, little by little, the game began to make sense.

This chapter describes some important things to look for during a football game. Give yourself ample time to locate them either in the football stadium or on your television screen. Do it before the game starts if you are attending a game, because we all know what happens after the game begins; with the noise of the football fans, and the action taking place on the field, it might be difficult for you to focus on the specific items listed here. It will probably be a confusing experience at first; just remember, it will get easier.

ST. JOHN OF MADDEN

If you decide to watch a game on a Sunday afternoon, you may find several games being televised at the same time. Which one should you choose to watch? Aren't they all pretty much the same? I don't think so. My advice is to watch the game that **St. John of Madden** is announcing. Saint who? Let me explain.

John Madden, a former NFL coach with the Oakland Raiders, was a sportscaster for CBS Sports for 13 years. He has made professional football into an enjoyable as well as educational spectator activity. Not only is John Madden an expert in professional football, he explains the action on the field in a way that can be appreciated by fanatic and novice alike. I believe that people who want to know more about the game can learn a great deal just by listening to his anecdotes and descriptions, and by watching him illustrate football maneuvers on his electronic chalkboard, which shows up on your television screen.

By making the game understandable, I believe that Madden makes an enormous contribution to the public's understanding of football. He was partnered at CBS Sports with a former NFL player, Pat Summerall; together they made up what I consider to be the best announcing team in the world of sports.

In addition to his broadcasting duties, for the past ten years Madden has chosen a select group of NFL players to be on his **"All Madden"** team. Through this ritual, he makes football fun for participants and spectators alike; at the end of each year, both fans and players eagerly anticipate the announcement of the newest members of the All Madden team. Although this selection does not go into the NFL record books, the players are nevertheless honored to be members of the chosen few.

I was quoted in a newspaper article one time as stating that John Madden was my idol and that he should be canonized. After reading this article about my feelings toward Madden and my recommendation for his elevation to sainthood, a local television anchorman dubbed him St. John of Madden.

So whenever you can, take my advice and watch St. John of Madden. Sometimes I have been really lucky on a Sunday: when Madden broadcasts a New York Giants game, it's two treats in one! You'll love his interesting stories, explanations and illustrations, and trust me, you'll learn a lot!

Beginning with the 1994-95 season, John Madden and Pat Summerall no longer announced games for CBS. For the first time in 38 years, CBS Sports did not broadcast NFL games in 1994-95. Madden and Summerall assumed broadcasting duties with the Fox Network. Be sure you tune in to see them – it's well worth it, as they further enliven the action on the football field.

FOOTBALL FIELD

The **football field** measures 120 yards long by 53⅓ yards wide, and it is sometimes called a **gridiron** because the pattern of yard lines resembles a grate upon which food is cooked over a fire. The field is made of either natural grass or artificial turf called **Astro Turf.** You can identify the field's surface by just looking at it. If it isn't obvious at first, pay special attention when the players get tackled. If the field is natural grass, their uniforms will be dirty and grass stained by the end of the game. If it is Astro Turf, they will slide a lot further on the field.

Each NFL team has a full-time groundskeeping crew whose primary responsibility is keeping the football field in good playing condition. As you might expect, these groundskeepers do not take their work lightly. A large sign (created by a groundskeeper with a pleasant sense of humor) could be seen on the football field of Joe Robbie Stadium in Miami right before the start of Super Bowl XXIX. It read as follows:

"Attention: Please keep off the field. We have some new additions to our grass family quietly growing. They need peace and quiet. As you know, grass grows by inches and is killed by feet."

As you look at the football field, you may be wondering, "What do all those lines mean?" Look at the diagram below. Refer to the numbers on the diagram to help you identify the terms related to the football field.

- The main playing area is 100 yards long running from one **goal line** (4) to the other. The goal lines are considered to be inside the **end zones** (3).

- **End lines** (2): Boundary at each end of the field 10 yards behind the **goal lines** (4).

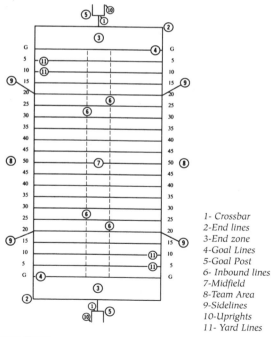

1- Crossbar
2-End lines
3-End zone
4-Goal Lines
5-Goal Post
6- Inbound lines
7-Midfield
8-Team Area
9-Sidelines
10-Uprights
11- Yard Lines

2.1 FOOTBALL FIELD

- **End zone** (3): Area 10 yards deep located at each end of the field. Touchdowns, safeties and 2-point conversions are scored here.

- **Goal post** (5): Shiny, gold-colored, Y-shaped structure that stands 10 yards behind each **goal line** (4) and is centered on the **end line** (2). Consists of a padded curved base, two vertical poles called **uprights** (10) connected by an 18-foot, 6-inch horizontal **crossbar** (1). The crossbar is 10 feet above the ground, while the uprights extend 30 feet above the crossbar. Attached behind the goal post is a large net that is raised behind the uprights whenever an extra point or field goal is attempted. The net prevents the kicked football from going into the stands. The NFL requires the nets not so much because of the cost of footballs going into the crowd, but more so to reduce the number of times fans fight over the kicked football.

- **Sidelines** (9): The lines at the sides of the field and the areas beyond them. Any player who touches or crosses a sideline is considered to be out of bounds.

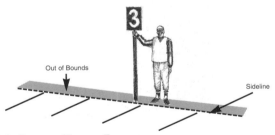

Out of Bounds

Sideline

2.2 SIDELINE/OUT OF BOUNDS

- **Yard lines** (11): Also called **stripes**, lines parallel to the **goal lines** (4), which extend across the width of the field from **sideline** (9) to sideline. The field is marked every five yards by yard lines that indicate the distance to the nearest goal line. The numbers on the playing field show the yard lines in multiples of ten.

Between the 5-yard stripes are other lines one yard apart, which assist officials in accurately placing the ball in preparation for a new play once the previous play has been completed.

Yards are numbered from each goal line (4) toward the middle of the field (goal line, 5-yard line, 10-yard line, 15-yard line, etc.). The 50-yard line, also called **midfield** (7), divides the field into two parts. Once a team advances the ball to midfield, further advancement is described by a **decrease** of 5 yards rather than an increase, as the team moves towards its opponent's goal line. Therefore, in football jargon, you will never hear of a team being on any yard line greater than the 50-yard line.

Look carefully and you will see a solid line one yard long located two yards from the middle of each goal line. This line indicates the area where the ball is placed for either a 1-point or 2-point conversion attempt.

- **Team Areas** (8): Areas between the 35-yard lines of the field where players, coaching staff, and other team personnel are located during a game.

- **Inbound Lines and Hashmarks** (6): Inbound lines are dotted lines parallel to the sidelines, and cross the yard lines 70' 9" from each sideline. Hashmarks are lines one yard apart that extend from one goal line to the other, parallel to the yard lines, perpendicular to the center, and located on both sidelines and inbound lines. Inbound lines and hashmarks are used to assist the officials in spotting or placing the football to start a new play if the ball goes out of bounds or lands on the sidelines on a previous play. (see Diagram 2.3)

If the previous play ends with the ball going out of bounds, for example, on the 4-yard line (X) or in the area between the right hashmarks and the right sideline on the 4-yard line, the official brings the ball to the nearest (in this case, the right) hashmark and "spots" it on the 4-yard line (Y). If the play ends with the ball between the right and left inbound lines/hashmarks, it stays there for the new play.

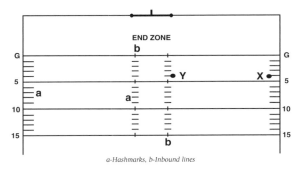

a-Hashmarks, b-Inbound lines

2.3 INBOUND LINES AND HASHMARKS

By using the hashmark system of placing the ball, the players have more room to run plays to both sides of the field instead of being restricted to only the area near the sidelines.

- **Red Zone** - Although it is not specifically marked on the field, the "red zone" refers to the area between a defensive team's 20-yard line and its goal line. You hear the term used when the offense is in that end of the field and is close to scoring.

- **Pylons** - These are flags on flexible poles that are located in each of the corners of the end zones.

- **Second Clock** - There are two identical clocks located at either end of the playing field which are used for the timing of individual plays. At the end of each play, these clocks are set at 40 seconds; the offense must start a new play before these 40 seconds have expired, or it can be penalized for delay of game.

- **Down Marker** - This is a 4-foot pole located on the sidelines with four signs numbered 1, 2, 3 and 4 that are flipped over at the start of each play. The down marker marks the most forward point of the ball at every play and displays the number of the down.

- **Scoreboard** - A large board in the stadium that displays the following information:
  - the score
  - yards to go for a first down
  - the down
  - the quarter *(period)*
  - the teams
  - time remaining in the quarter *(official clock)*
  - time outs remaining for each team
  - team with the ball

Pay attention to the scoreboard! It is a valuable source of information for you during a game. Every once in a while you may hear a roar from the crowd and wonder why it happened since nothing particularly exciting was going on in the field at the time. It is possible that the fans are reacting to other NFL game scores that are periodically posted on the scoreboard.

EQUIPMENT AND UNIFORMS

My mother used to ask my father, "I just don't understand. Why do these big football players have such little rear ends?" Very simply, the buttocks area is one of the few parts of the player's anatomy that isn't heavily padded. The padding on the shoulders, thighs, ribs, and hips makes these areas appear larger.

Protective equipment helps to prevent injuries. The function or position of a player determines how much equipment he wears. Some players tend to wear a lot of padding because they are involved in the most physical contact through tackling and blocking; others wear less protective equipment so that they can move more easily and run at top speed.

Over all of this protective equipment, which can add 15 to 20 pounds of extra weight to the player, is the uniform, which consists of a shirt called a jersey and

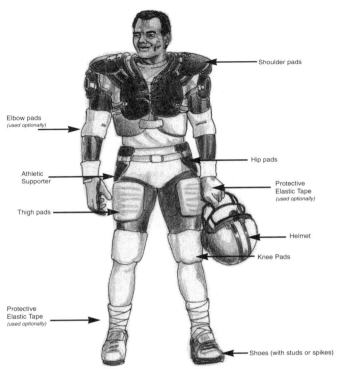

Shoulder pads

Elbow pads
(used optionally)

Hip pads

Athletic
Supporter

Protective
Elastic Tape
(used optionally)

Thigh pads

Helmet

Knee Pads

Protective
Elastic Tape
(used optionally)

Shoes (with studs or spikes)

2.4 FOOTBALL PLAYER - EQUIPMENT

pants of contrasting colors that are tightly fitted so that opposing players cannot easily grasp them when trying to tackle. The player's number is displayed on the front, back and sleeves of his jersey as well as on the back of his helmet for identification by the officials and spectators.

Opposing teams must wear jerseys of contrasting colors, and neither team is allowed to wear a uniform of a color similar to a football. Every team has two sets of uniforms, one of which is usually white. The team uses one uniform when it plays on its home field, the other of another color when it plays away from home. According to NFL rules, the home team has the choice of uniform and must notify its opponent of that choice. Prior to its first game, each team chooses which of its uniforms it will wear at home during the entire season. If it chooses its team color, then the visiting team has to wear its white jersey; if the team chooses white to wear at home, then each visiting team has to wear its team color.

2.5 PLAYER IN UNIFORM

The NFL takes rules about uniforms and equipment quite seriously. Now the NFL plans to get tough with players who don't conform to the league's dress code: those players whose uniforms don't conform will not be allowed to play. Throughout the years, there has been controversy about the way in which players have dressed for football games.

The dress code policy is nothing new. Back in the 1970's, Fred Biletnikoff and Mike Siani, receivers for the Oakland Raiders, were threatened with fines by the NFL because they didn't pull their uniform socks all the way up. Biletnikoff and Siani informed League officials that the reason they failed to pull their socks up was because they had skin conditions on their ankles that could be aggravated by keeping the area covered.

Another Raider player also had problems with the League concerning his appearance during a game. Dave Casper, a tight end, was fined $250 for not tucking in his

16

shirt during a game against the Pittsburgh Steelers. Casper sent the League a check for $62.50, one quarter of the fine, with an explanation of his side of the story: the remaining $187.50 of the fine, Casper asserted, should be assessed against the Pittsburgh Steelers because *they* were the ones who kept pulling his shirt out during the game. Casper received a note from then-Commissioner Pete Rozelle, saying that a viewing of the tape proved Casper right: the Steelers' defense *had* been pulling his shirt out, and the League accepted his fine of $62.50.

At the conclusion of the 1994-95 season, NFL officials began to discuss whether they would allow players to continue to wear bandannas. *USA Today* (June 13, 1995) reported that the NFL decided to drop the bandanna issue; the NFL may continue to supply bandannas as long as they match the team's predominant color. So keep an eye out for Deion Sanders of the Dallas Cowboys and Rickey Watters of the Philadelphia Eagles, two of the National Football League's most renowned bandanna-wearing players.

FOOTBALL

2.6 FOOTBALL

A football is prolate spheroid (oval-shaped), pointed at each end, consisting of a rubber bladder encased in pebble-grained leather and inflated with air. It has leather laces on one side to provide a good grip for holding and passing. The ball must be a "Wilson" and must bear the National Football League stamp and the signature of the NFL Commissioner. Regulation footballs must weigh between 14 and 15 ounces. To comply with League requirements, the home team must provide 24 footballs for officials' testing two hours before the game begins.

It is popularly called the **pigskin,** probably because footballs were first made of pigskin.

OFFICIALS

2.7 OFFICIAL

There is a seven-member officiating crew that makes sure that the game is played according to the rules. Each official has particular duties, but any of the officials may call a rule violation. The officials' uniform consists of white pants, a black and white striped shirt, and a black cap with white stripes. Each of the officials also has a number on his back for identification purposes. The **referee,** the chief official, wears a white cap and a wireless microphone and has the final word on all rulings.

You will also notice another crew positioned on the sidelines. This crew is known as the **chain crew/gang** and is responsible for the **down marker** and the **yardage chain.** Members of the chain crew/gang wear white shirts with either striped or solid colored vests.

ROSTER

If you are attending a professional football game, you may want to purchase a program. In it, among other things, you will find a **roster** listing names, positions, and other player information. A team is allowed to carry 53 players on its roster, with 45 eligible to play and eight spots reserved for inactive players.

TEAM ROSTER

NO.	NAME	POS.	HT./WT.	YRS. PRO	SCHOOL
60	Theo Adams	G	6-5/300	3	Hawaii
77	Oliver Barnett	DE	6-3/285	6	Kentucky
79	Harris Barton	G	6-4/286	9	North Carolina
4	Doug Brien	K	5-11/177	2	California
96	Dennis Brown	DE	6-4/280	6	Washington
86	Brett Carolan	TE	6-3/241	2	Washington State
76	Jason Childs	T	6-4/292	2	North Dakota
91	Shane Collins	DE	6-3/267	6	Arizona State
67	Chris Dalman	G/C	6-3/285	3	Stanford
25	Eric Davis	CB	5-11/178	6	Jacksonville State
63	Derrick Deese	G	6-3/270	4	USC
33	Dedrick Dodge	S	6-2/184	4	Florida State
22	Tyronne Drakeford	CB	5-9/185	2	Virginia Tech
40	William Floyd	FB	6-1/242	2	Florida State
14	Bob Gagliano	QB	6-3/205	10	Utah State
59	Steve Gordon	C	6-4/290	2	California
18	Elvis Grbac	QB	6-5/232	3	Michigan
36	Merton Hanks	CB	6-2/185	5	Iowa
47	Clifford Hicks	S/CB	5-10/187	8	Oregon
84	Brent Jones	TE	6-4/230	9	Santa Clara
58	Todd Kelly	DE	6-2/259	3	Tennessee
20	Derek Loville	RB	5-10/205	4	Oregon
29	Anthony Lynn	RB	6-3/230	2	Texas Tech
46	Tim McDonald	S	6-2/215	9	USC
69	Rod Milstead	G	6-2/290	4	Delaware State
55	Kevin Mitchell	LB	6-1/260	2	Syracuse
31	Derrick Moore	RB	6-1/227	3	NE Oklahoma St.
51	Ken Norton, Jr.	LB	6-2/241	8	UCLA
66	Bart Oates	C	6-3/278	11	Brigham Young
53	Anthony Peterson	LB	6-0/223	2	Notre Dame
50	Gary Plummer	LB	6-2/247	10	California
23	Marquez Pope	CB/S	5-11/193	4	Fresno State
85	Ted Popson	TE	6-4/250	2	Portland State
80	Jerry Rice	WR	6-2/200	11	Miss. Valley State
10	Patrick Rowe	WR	6-1/195	3	San Diego State
61	Jessie Sapolu	C	6-4/278	13	Hawaii
76	Kirk Scrafford	T	6-6/275	6	Montana
88	Nate Singleton	WR	5-11/190	4	Grambling
94	Dana Stubblefield	DT	6-2/302	3	Kansas
64	Ralph Tamm	G	6-4/280	8	West Chester
82	John Taylor	WR	6-1/185	10	Delaware State
	Tommy Thompson	P	5-10/192	1	Oregon
71	Jim Wahler	DT	6-4/275	6	UCLA
27	Adam Walker	RB	6-1/210	3	Pittsburgh
74	Steve Wallace	T	6-5/280	10	Auburn
92	Troy Wilson	DE	6-4/235	3	Pitt. St. (Kansas)
54	Lee Woodall	LB	6-0/220	2	West Chester
97	Bryant Young	DT	6-2/276	2	Notre Dame
8	Steve Young	QB	6-2/205	11	Brigham Young

1995 DRAFT CHOICES

RD.	NAME	POS.	HT./WT.	SCHOOL
1	J.J. Stokes	WR	6-4/217	UCLA
4	Tim Hanshaw	G	6-5/300	Brigham Young
6	Antonio Armstrong	LB	6-1/285	Texas A&M
7	Herbert Coleman	DE	6-1/290	Trinity International

2.8 TEAM ROSTER: SAN FRANCISCO 49ERS

Rosters can be organized alphabetically or numerically. Generally, you will find the player's name, number, position, height, weight, birthdate, the college he attended, and the number of years of NFL experience he has. Sometimes rosters list the names of the coaching staff, and game programs often list the names and identification numbers of the game's officiating crew.

To make reading the roster (Figure 2.8) easier, let me give you a list of the different abbreviations for player positions that may be used. I will be describing all of these player positions later.

Special Team		Offense		Defense	
PK	Place Kicker	QB	Quarterback	NT	Nose Tackle
K	Kicker	FB	Fullback	DE	Defensive End
P	Punter	HB	Halfback	DT	Defensive Tackle
KR	Kick Returner	RB	Running Back	RE	Right End
PR	Punt Returner	WR	Wide Receiver	LE	Left End
		FL	Flanker	LB	Linebacker
		C	Center	RILB	Right Inside Linebacker
		LG	Left Guard	ROLB	Right Outside Linebacker
		RG	Right Guard	LILB	Left Inside Linebacker
		T	Tackle	LOLB	Left Outside Linebacker
				MLB	Middle Linebacker
				CB	Cornerback
				LCB	Left Cornerback
				RCB	Right Cornerback
				DB	Defensive Back
				S	Safety
				FS	Free Safety
				SS	Strong Safety

Each player has a specific role on the team and is assigned a jersey number according to that role to help the spectators and officials identify him. Player numbers, as required by the NFL, are assigned in the following way:

Position	Number
Quarterbacks	1-19
Kickers	1-19
Punters	1-19
Running Backs	20-49
Defensive Backs	20-49
Centers	50-59
Linebackers	50-59
Defensive Linemen	60-79
Offensive Linemen	60-79
Wide Receivers	80-89
Tight Ends	80-89
Some Defensive Linemen	90-99
Some Linebackers	90-99

Try to become familiar with this numbering system; it will help you to identify the particular functions of the players. Once you understand this system, you'll be able to identify the position of a particular player as soon as he walks onto the field.

TEAM SCHEDULES

Your program may also have team schedules that list dates, opponents, and sometimes the scores. On a team's schedule (in this case, the New York Jets schedule), all its home games are written in capital letters. All its **away** games (games played away from home) are written in lower case letters and may sometimes have the word **at** preceding the team's name. Therefore, a Jets' NFL schedule might show the following entries:

a. **September 13   DALLAS   W 27-20**
   The Jets played at home against the Dallas Cowboys on September 13 and won 27 to 20.

b. **October 15 Philadelphia   L 17-14 OT**
   The Jets played the Philadelphia Eagles in Philadelphia and lost the game 17 to 14 in overtime (OT).

c. **November 14 at Washington**
   The Jets will play the Washington Redskins in Washington on November 14.

If you ever see **BYE** written on the schedule, it means an **off date**; in other words, it is a date that the team is not scheduled to play.

Although I have briefly identified some things you should look for during a game, there will be more details for you to follow in later chapters. It's important for you to familiarize yourself with these items and the proper terminology to use when discussing them. But now let's move on to discuss the main reason for football's great popularity: the players.

✔ CHAPTER 2 CHECKLIST
THINGS TO REMEMBER

- Field – 120 yds x 53⅓ yds – made of grass or artificial turf (Astro Turf)
- Playing area 100 yards long
- Y-shaped goal post
- End zone – touchdowns and safeties are scored here
- Hashmarks – used to "spot" the ball
- Referee – chief official

TERMS TO KNOW

BYE	gang	pigskin	roster
chain	gridiron	pylon	stripes

EXTRA POINTS: DID YOU KNOW?

According to **The Official Pro Football Hall of Fame Answer Book**, Astro Turf first appeared on the football scene in 1966. The individuals building the Astro Dome in Houston, Texas, discovered that natural grass wouldn't grow under glass in a domed stadium. They had to install a synthetic carpetlike playing surface, commonly known today as Astro Turf.

CHAPTER 3

PLAYERS: WHO DOES WHAT?

"Split ends? Why would anyone want to have split ends?"
- Mary B. (1988)

People who are learning the game of football often ask about the location of the ball during the game. To them, football appears to involve a bunch of big guys moving forward on the field, stopping and falling, followed by getting up, moving a bit, stopping and falling again. Novice viewers complain that it's confusing to follow the action of the game; they don't know where the ball is or the specific functions of each player. They want to know which player does what on a football team.

This chapter, which is divided into the three sections of **offense, defense** and **special teams**, gives you a brief description of each player's position, where he lines up, and the specific role he plays. For readers who are unsure about the specific responsibilities of the players, this discussion should help clear up some of your confusion.

Although football is played with 11 players on each side, teams have many more members than that. As you already know, NFL teams are allowed to have 53 players on a roster, 45 who are eligible to play and eight spots for inactive players. Each player on the team has a particular position and plays a specific role; he may be a member of the starting lineup (the **first string**) or may be a substitute or **backup.** Since a full football team is made up of offense, defense, and special teams, each player's position described in this chapter is grouped according to these three categories.

I. OFFENSE

The offense is made up of seven **linemen** and four **backs.** There must always be at least seven offensive players on or within a foot of the **line of scrimmage**, the spot on the field where the offense has the ball. There will be much more discussion about the line of scrimmage in the next chapter.

LINEMEN

The offensive line consists of five **interior linemen** and two **ends**. The interior linemen, also called **offensive linemen**, take a crouched stance on the line of scrimmage. When the ball is snapped, they block the opposing defensive linemen, keeping them away from the ball carrier and their quarterback. The interior line, which is usually made up of the five biggest offensive players (often weighing more than 300 pounds, earning the nickname "Meat on the Hoof"), consists of a **center**, two **guards**, and two **tackles**.

A good way to remember the positions of the interior linemen is to keep in mind they are organized alphabetically from the middle of the line towards the end: Center – Guard – Tackle. These players are not designated as **eligible receivers**, meaning that they are not allowed to catch passes unless they report a change in their eligibility status to the officials before a particular play.

Another thing to remember about some player positions is that they are described by the terms "left" and "right." "Left" and "right" refer to what side of the football the players position themselves at the beginning of each play. Therefore, a **left guard (LG)** is a guard who lines up on the left side of the football.

3.1 OFFENSIVE LINEMAN

Center (C)
- Also called the snapper
- Jersey numbers 50-59
- Snaps or **hikes** the football behind to the quarterback, punter, or other offensive player
- Provides blocking and protects the quarterback

Guard (G)
- Sometimes referred to as left guard (LG) and right guard (RG)
- Jersey numbers 60-69
- Provides blocking interference for running backs and protection for the quarterback

Tackle (T)
- Sometimes referred to as left tackle (LT) and right tackle (RT)
- Jersey numbers 60-69
- Provides blocking protection for the quarterback and blocking for running backs

End

Each of the two ends plays a position on the outside of the interior linemen. One of the jobs of the ends, like that of the interior linemen, is to block. However, unlike interior linemen, ends may catch passes and occasionally even carry the ball. Football teams usually have two types of ends: the **tight end** and the **split end** or **wide receiver**.

Tight end (TE)
- Strongest of all receivers
- Jersey numbers 80-89

The tight end lines up **tight** to the interior linemen next to the tackle. He serves as a pass receiver and has important blocking responsibilities. Occasionally, teams use two tight ends in their formations.

Split end (SE)
- Sometimes called **wide receiver (WR)** or **wideout**
- Jersey numbers 80-89

Receivers line up **wide away** from the interior linemen on the line of scrimmage. They primarily catch passes, although they are eligible to run with the ball or sometimes act as decoys to lure defenders away from the ball carrier. These players are usually the speediest members of the team and line up far to one side of the field.

Two terms you may hear during a game: **weak side** and **strong side**. Refer to Diagram 3.3 to assist in making sense out of the following discussion.

Weak side refers to the side where the split end (wide receiver) lines up. This is opposite the ball from the tight end's side. Since the split end (SE) or wide receiver (WR) lines up several yards away from his tackle, he creates an open space or a **weakness** in the

3.2 Receiver

line. The weak side may be more easily attacked by the defense.

Strong side refers to the side of the offensive line where the tight end (TE) lines up. Since the tight end lines up "tight" to the tackle, there is no open space or weak area for the defense to penetrate.

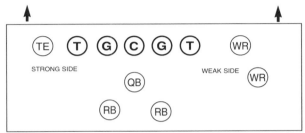

QB- *Quarterback, C-Center, TE-Tight End, G-Guard, T-Tackle, RB-Running Back, WR-Wide Receiver*

3.3 OFFENSIVE LINE

This diagram shows the offensive line that is made up of the interior linemen and two ends. Remember, there must be at least seven offensive players on the line of scrimmage when the ball is snapped. The remaining players on the offensive team are members of the backfield.

BACKS

The **backfield** is the unit which positions itself behind or in back of the offensive linemen, at least one yard behind the line of scrimmage. There are usually four offensive backs: the quarterback, running backs and receivers (they catch passes but sometimes line up behind the line of scrimmage). On the offense, the **backs** are the players who are allowed to carry the ball.

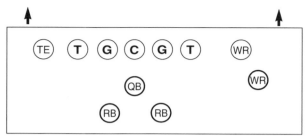

QB- Quarterback, C-Center, TE-Tight End, G-Guard, T-Tackle, RB-Running Back, WR-Wide Receiver

3.4 OFFENSIVE BACKFIELD

Quarterback (QB)

- Offensive leader and signal caller
- Jersey numbers 1-19
- Lines up directly behind the **center (C)** to receive the football

The quarterback directs the offense, is the primary passer and ball handler, and occasionally runs with the ball. He calls out the signals known as the **cadence** to let the rest of the team know when the ball will be snapped to start a play. When he gets the ball, he can pass it downfield to a teammate, give it to one of the other backs by a direct handoff or a **lateral** (a short, underhand pass to the side), or keep the ball himself and run with it.

3.5 QUARTERBACK

Running Back (RB)

- **Halfback (HB):** Jersey numbers 20-29, 40-49
- **Fullback (FB):** Jersey numbers 30-39
- **Flanker (FL):** Jersey numbers 20-49

Most backfields have a halfback and a fullback, although both of them may be designated simply as **running backs**. Running backs run with the ball, obviously, but are also allowed to catch passes. These backs, who usually line up behind the quarterback (QB), are at least one yard behind the line of scrimmage in the area known as the **backfield**. You may come across other terms such as **setback, tailback (TB), slotback (SB)**, and **wingback (WB)**, but they all refer to running backs.

The **halfback**, usually the smaller and quicker of the backs, runs with the ball, catches passes, blocks, and sometimes may even throw a pass.

The **fullback**, who is bigger than the halfback, and who lines up on the same side as the tight end, is used primarily for blocking and short runs into the defensive line.

The **flanker** is a back who lines up at least one yard behind the line of scrimmage on the same side as the tight end and is eligible to either run with the ball or catch passes.

Diagram 3.6 shows the entire 11-member offensive team. The dotted circle indicates where a quarterback

3.6 ENTIRE 11-MAN OFFENSE IN SHOTGUN FORMATION

lines up in a **shotgun formation**. A shotgun formation is a formation in which the quarterback takes the center snap at least five yards behind the center, instead of from directly behind him.

Just remember that some players, such as the offensive linemen, line up in virtually the same way every time; but other players line up differently depending upon the particular offensive game plan (e.g., sometimes you will see two running backs, sometimes three; sometimes one tight end, sometimes two).

Now let's move on to the **defense**, the group of players that defends its goal. The defense lines up opposite the offense (the team that has the football).

II. DEFENSE

The defensive team is divided into three groups: (1) **defensive linemen**; (2) **linebackers**; and (3) **defensive backs**, also referred to as the **secondary** or **defensive backfield**. The number of players in each group depends upon the defensive formation or **alignment** the team is using. Alignments, which can vary from play to play, are formed in response to what the defense thinks the offense is going to do.

DEFENSIVE LINEMEN (also called **down linemen**)

• Defensive End (DE)

• Guard (Nosetackle – NT)

• Defensive Tackle (DT)

• Jersey numbers 60-79

The defensive line, which is sometimes called the **front four** and usually has three or four of the largest players on the defensive team, may have as many players as it chooses. Usual alignments, however, call for three to six defensive linemen to face the offense at the line of scrimmage.

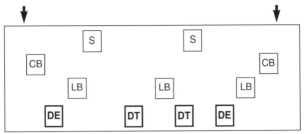

DT-Defensive Tackle, DE-Defensive End, LB-Linebacker, S-Safety, CB-Cornerback

3.7 DEFENSIVE LINE
This diagram shows the defense with a four-man defensive line, sometimes called the "front four."

A three-man line consists of a **middle guard**, also called a **nose tackle** (NT), and two ends (DE). A five-man line consists of a middle guard, two tackles (DT) and two ends (DE). Defensive linemen attempt to push past the offensive linemen to tackle ball carriers. They also keep pressure on the quarterback so that he hurries his passes or is **sacked**, that is, he gets tackled behind the line of scrimmage.

LINEBACKERS (LB)

• Jersey numbers 50-59

Linebackers position themselves 2 or 3 yards behind the linemen, or sometimes move up alongside them. If the offense tries a running play, the linebackers move up and try to tackle the ball carriers. If the offense attempts a pass play, the linebackers move back to help the defensive backs cover the pass receivers or rush the quarterback in an attempt to sack him.

3.8 LINEBACKER

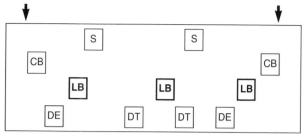

DT-Defensive Tackle, DE-Defensive End, LB-Linebackers, S-Safety, CB-Cornerback

3.9 DEFENSIVE LINE
This diagram shows three linebackers lined up behind the defensive front line.

A team that uses a four-man defensive line will normally have three linebackers. The player who lines up facing the center (C) is the middle linebacker (MLB). The two other players called outside linebackers (OLB) stand outside the defensive ends. Four linebackers are used with a three-man line, and two are used with a five-man line.

DEFENSIVE BACKFIELD

The defensive backfield, also called the **secondary**, is made up of two **cornerbacks** and two **safeties**. These players are also called **defensive backs**. The chief task of the secondary is to defend against the offense's passing attack. However, if ball carriers get past the defensive linemen and linebackers, the defensive backs must make the tackles. Defensive backs must be fast enough to cover speedy pass receivers while also being good **open field** (one-on-one) tacklers; that is, be able to tackle an opponent and bring him to the ground in an open space on the field without any help from their teammates. Speed, timing, and concentration are probably the most important traits for a defensive back to possess.

Cornerback (CB)

• Jersey numbers 20-49

The cornerbacks stand 8 to 10 yards behind the line of scrimmage at the corners of the defensive formation. Their primary responsibility is to prevent wide receivers from catching short passes on the two corner areas of the field near the sidelines.

Safety (S)

• Jersey numbers 20-49

The safeties play 8 to 12 yards behind the line of scrimmage. Their primary responsibility is to prevent wide receivers from catching long passes in the middle of the field. There are two types of safeties: a **free safety**, sometimes called the **weak safety**, and a **strong safety**.

The **free safety (FS)** usually lines up in the middle of the field between the cornerbacks. Some of his responsibilities include making adjustments in the defensive secondary's coverage in response to the offensive formation and assisting the cornerbacks in providing pass coverage.

The **strong safety (SS)** lines up on the same side of the field as the offensive team's tight end. His major responsibility is providing pass defense against the tight end.

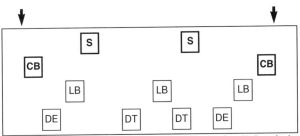

DT-Defensive Tackle, DE-Defensive End, LB-Linebackers, S-Safety, CB-Cornerback

3.10 ENTIRE 11-MAN DEFENSE

III. SPECIAL TEAMS

In addition to the offensive and defensive units, a football team includes **special teams**. These are the units that go on to the field in kicking situations (kickoffs, kickoff returns, punts, punt returns, extra points, and field goals). Some players play on both the offense and a special team, the defense and a special team, or on one or more special teams.

In these kicking situations, who does the actual kicking? Depending upon the specific situation, either one of the kicking specialists, the **kicker** or the **punter**, kicks the ball.

Although they are both kickers, they do not do the same job.

Kicker (K) or Placekicker (PK)

• Jersey Numbers 1-19

The kicker or placekicker is part of the special team who comes on the field for extra points, kickoffs, and field goals. For kickoffs, he puts the ball into play by a placekick with the use of a kicking tee. In other kicking situations, such as for extra points and field goals, a teammate called the **holder** holds the ball for the kicker. Backup quarterbacks usually act as the holders on a team because they have good ball handling skills and a lot of experience taking snaps during practice.

3.11 PLACEKICKER AND HOLDER

Punter (P)

• Jersey Numbers 1-19

The punter is the player who kicks the ball by first dropping it, then kicking before it hits the ground. When a punter is called onto the field, his duty is to kick the ball as far into the receiving team's territory as possible. He stands about 15 yards behind the line of scrimmage; the center, sometimes called the **long snapper** in kicking situations, snaps the ball directly back to him. A good punter makes sure that the laces on the football are facing up, drops the ball, then kicks it off the top of his foot as quickly as possible before it hits the ground.

3.12 PUNTER

The punter tries to keep his kick in the air as long as possible, so his teammates can run downfield and tackle the opponent, known as the **punt returner**, who catches the ball. The number of seconds that elapse between the time the punter kicks the ball and the punt returner catches it is called the **hang time**. When a punter punts the ball, watch your television screen. Sometimes you will see a clock counting off seconds to calculate the punter's hang time. The longer the hang time, the better it is for the punting team.

Kick Returner (KR)/
Punt Returner (PR)

Kick return specialists are also members of special teams. They are designated as the players who catch punts or kickoffs and try to advance them in the direction of their opponent's goal line. They may also serve as running backs, wide receivers, or defensive backs throughout most of the game. Punt returners and kick returners have to have good ball handling skills and be very quick to avoid oncoming tacklers.

3.13 KICK RETURNER/PUNT KICKER

This brief description of player positions should help you in understanding that football players do not line up randomly, but each player has a specific role in each and every play. Try to become familiar with these positions and refer to the diagrams as often as you need to for help. Although players who play certain positions such as quarterback, running back, and wide receiver tend to get most of the media's attention, each player makes a significant contribution to the overall success of the team.

CHAPTER 3 CHECKLIST
THINGS TO REMEMBER

Offense
Offensive Lineman (OL)
Center (C)
Guard (G)
Tackle (T)
Tight End (TE)
Quarterback (QB)
Wide Receiver (WR)
Running Back (RB)
Flanker (FL)

Defense
Defensive End (DE)
Guard (G)
Defensive Tackle (DT)
Linebacker (LB)
Defensive Back (DB)
Cornerback (CB)
Safety (S)
Nose Tackle (NT)

Special Teams
Kicker (K)
Placekicker (PK)
Punter (P)
Kick Returner (KR)
Punt Returner (PR)

SPECIAL TEAMS

extra point
field goal

kick return
kickoff

punt return
punting

TERMS TO KNOW

alignment
cadence
down linemen
front four

hang time
hike
holder
long snapper

snap
strong side
weak side

EXTRA POINTS: DID YOU KNOW?

The terms **fullback**, **halfback**, and **quarterback** were all derived from the way players in the past lined up at the line of scrimmage. The fullback lined up all the way ("full way") behind the line of scrimmage; the halfback lined up halfway between the line of scrimmage and the fullback; the quarterback lined up a "quarter of the way" back between the line of scrimmage and the fullback. Nowadays, the running backs (halfback and fullback) generally line up next to, rather than behind, each other.

CHAPTER 4

How Football is Played

"What does hiking have to do with football?" - Margaret D. (1990)

Now that you have briefly familiarized yourself with the field, equipment, scoring, and players, let's take a look at how all are related. This chapter discusses fundamentals, common football strategies, and how the football is moved up and down the field during a game.

TIMING OF THE GAME

The action in a football game is not continuous as it is in baseball, hockey, and other sports. When the ball is not in play, the **official clock** is stopped. The official clock is also stopped when a runner goes out of bounds, when passes are incomplete, or after a team scores.

Professional football teams are allowed 40 seconds between the end of one play to the time when the ball is snapped to start the next play. There are also 25-second intervals after certain administrative stoppages and game delays. These 40/25 second intervals are timed by the **second clock** or **play clock**.

Both teams are allowed three time outs per half of one minute and 50 seconds each. Time outs are used not so much as rest periods for the players as opportunities to rally the team and consult with the coaches near the end of the first half or the end of the game. Timeouts are commonly used to stop the clock between plays, giving the team who called the time out more time to score points or to gain possession of the ball. There are also time outs called by the officials for technical reasons such as television commercial breaks. Since these are officials' time outs, they are not counted as a time out for either team.

METHODS OF SCORING

As previously mentioned, the object of the game of football is to score more points than the opposing team within the regulation time of play. In professional football, if both teams have scored the same number of points at the end of the second half, it is a **tie**. The teams must then play an overtime period called **sudden death** in which the first team to score is declared the winner.

A football team can score points in five different ways:

1. Touchdown (6 points)

A team scores a **touchdown** when a player carries the ball beyond the opponent's goal line or when the ball is passed to a player who catches it in the opponent's end zone. The defense scores a touchdown if it recovers a **fumble** (a ball dropped by the offense) in its opponent's end zone, or carries a recovered fumble into its opponent's end

4.1 OFFICIAL SIGNALING TOUCHDOWN

zone. The defense also earns a touchdown if it catches (**intercepts**) a pass intended for an offensive player and carries that pass (an **interception**) into the offensive team's end zone.

2. Conversion/extra point (1 point)

After a team scores a touchdown, it is permitted to try for a **conversion**, which is an additional point. While time is called out, the ball is placed on the 2-yard line of the defensive team. The center then snaps it back several yards behind the line of scrimmage to a **holder**, usually someone with excellent ball handling skills such as the quarterback. The holder sets the ball on its point on the ground, and the kicker kicks the ball over the crossbar of the goal post. After scoring a touchdown and an extra point, the scoring team then kicks off to its opponent. Even if the extra point attempt is not successful, the kicking team still must give up possession of the ball by kicking off to the other team.

3. Conversion (2 points)

After a team scores a touchdown, it also has the option of attempting a 2-point rather than a 1-point conversion. Like the 1-point conversion, the ball is placed on the defense's 2-yard line. The team can score 2 points by either running or passing the ball into the defense's end zone. As in the case with the 1-point conversion, the scoring team must kick off to the opponent even if the 2-point conversion attempt is unsuccessful.

4. Field goal (3 points)

A team scores a **field goal** by placekicking the ball over the crossbar of its opponent's goal post. As with the extra point attempt, the football is snapped back to the holder who is positioned on one knee and holds the ball for the kicker. Only the offense can attempt field goals. Although field goals may be attempted from anywhere on the field, teams generally attempt them only from within their opponent's 35-yard line.

5. Safety (2 points)

In the game of football, the term **"safety"** can mean either a method of scoring or a defensive backfield player. During a Football Basics class I asked, "What's a safety worth?" (2 points was the answer I was looking for.) But one of my new students answered, "What's a safety worth? Hmm.... My son was a safety on his high school football team, and he's worth everything to me!" A very different answer than what I expected! Therefore, for purposes of the following discussion, a safety refers to a method of scoring, *not* the player position.

A safety is the only way a team can score points without having possession of the ball. Therefore, the defense is the only team that can score a safety. A safety is scored when the defense causes the offense to end a play behind its own goal line while it is still in possession of the football.

Some examples of a safety: a defensive lineman tackles the quarterback in the offensive team's end zone; a ball carrier is stopped in his own end zone; a blocked punt goes out of the kicking team's end zone; an offensive player is guilty of holding another player in his own end zone; the quarterback intentionally throws the ball away while in his end zone. After the offense gives up a safety to the defense, it must turn the ball over to the other team. To do this, the offense must then kick the ball off from its own 20-yard line, but can choose to do so by means of either a punt or a placekick without a tee.

WATCH THE OFFICIALS! They signal whenever points are scored. Watch them carefully, especially in situations when a runner is trying to advance the football across his opponent's goal line and is stopped by several defensive players piling on top of him. Sometimes it is difficult to tell whether the ball carrier crosses the goal line (actually, whether the *ball* crosses the goal line),

41

since there are many defensive players intent on stopping him. If the runner crosses the goal line, the referee signals a touchdown by extending both of his arms directly above his head.

The referee uses this same signal when a team makes an extra point or a field goal.

4.2 SCORE

When a team scores a safety, the official places his palms together over his head.

4.4 SAFETY

If the team's attempt at an extra point or field goal is unsuccessful, the referee indicates "no good" by shifting his hands in a horizontal plane.

4.3 MISSED FIELD GOAL-EXTRA POINT

THE GAME

Before the game begins, the captains of the two teams meet with the referee at midfield for the **coin toss.** The captain of the visiting team has the honor of calling "heads" or "tails." The captain who wins the coin toss can either choose to have his team kick off (be the defense) or receive the kick (be the offense). The other team captain chooses which goal his team will defend. In most cases, teams choose to receive the opening kickoff in order to get the first chance at scoring. The team that loses the pre-game (first half) coin toss is allowed to make the choice at the beginning of the second half of the game.

4.5 PLACEKICKER

The game begins with a **kickoff**, a type of **free kick** in which the football is held upright by a kicking tee (with the laces facing away from the kicker) on the kicking team's 30-yard line. The kicker positions himself 10 yards behind the football and his teammates spread out in a straight line extending the width of the field. Because it is a free kick, members of the receiving team have to line up at least 10 yards away from the ball. After he raises his hand to indicate he is ready for the play to begin, the kicker runs up and kicks the ball as far down the field as possible. If the kicker kicks the ball out of bounds on the kickoff, his team is assessed a 5-yard penalty and he must re-kick from his own 25-yard line.

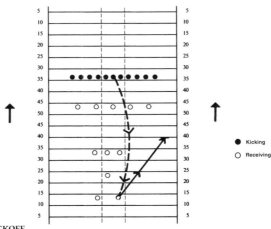

4.6 KICKOFF

As soon as the kicker kicks the ball off, his teammates run down the field as quickly as possible to stop the receiving team from advancing the ball. Once the **kick returner** catches the kickoff, he may run with the ball until he is tackled by any of his opponents and **downed. Tackling,** a defensive maneuver, involves using the hands and arms to stop or throw to the ground any opposing ball carrier. After a tackle is made, the referee blows his whistle to stop the play and places the ball on the spot where the ball carrier is downed – in other words, the place where his forward progress was stopped.

If the ball is kicked into the receiving team's end zone, the kick returner may do one of two things:

- He may catch the ball, run out of the end zone onto the playing field, and continue to run until he gets tackled.

- He may go down on one knee in the end zone ("downs the ball"), meaning that he will not attempt to step on the playing field. When this happens, it is called a **touchback** and the ball is automatically placed on the receiving team's 20-yard line for the next play.

Once the referee whistles the play dead, members of both the kicking team and receiving team (both members of special teams), leave the field. Then the offensive unit of the receiving team and the defensive unit of the kicking team take the field to begin the next series of plays.

Huddle

Once the offensive unit is organized, it begins a series of plays or **scrimmages** to move the ball in the direction of its opponent's goal line. The series of plays that a team puts together while keeping possession of the ball is called a **drive**. The location on the playing field that a team has reached is known as their **field position**. Before each play, you will notice the players getting together in a group on the field forming a circle called the **huddle.** In the huddle, the players decide on the strategy and signals for the next play. Generally, the quarterback is the one to tell his team which play will be used next in advancing the ball. Both the offensive and defensive teams have huddles. Sometimes a quarterback will use a **no huddle offense** to give his opponents less time to prepare, and consequently they are often caught off guard. Some teams are known for their "no huddle offense," as they frequently plan plays ahead of time without benefit of a discussion in a huddle.

4.7 HUDDLE

Teams usually have dozens of well-rehearsed basic plays and variations of these plays that they use during a game. Each play is designated by a series of code numbers or words called **signals.** The quarterback transmits these signals to his team while in the huddle since he is the player who directs the offense. Sometimes quarterbacks decide which plays to call; other times, the plays are selected by the offensive coordinator and the head coach. In the latter case, a substituted player can bring in the new play to the quarterback in the huddle, or players standing on the sidelines can use hand signals to transmit the play to the quarterback. In 1994, the NFL instituted a new radio system for the quarterback to communicate with the coaching staff on the sidelines.

The quarterback receives signals through a tiny unit inside his helmet. Some quarterbacks embrace the new system; others find that the radio transmission is an unnecessary distraction for them.

What types of information does the quarterback give to his teammates in the huddle?

Since the quarterback is responsible for making sure each of his teammates clearly understands the play and is in position in the 40 seconds from the end of one play to the beginning of a new one, he announces the new play in code. He usually includes the following information:

- The way the offense will line up (formation)
- The coded number of the running or passing play
- Whether there are any special blocking assignments to be done
- When the ball will be snapped (the cadence). The cadence (either a number or sound) is the last thing the quarterback yells to his teammates at the line of scrimmage before the ball is snapped and play begins.

Suppose the quarterback has called a play in the huddle, but when he and his offense line up, he **reads the defense**; in other words, he has noticed that the defense has recognized his formation and that his play has been anticipated. What can he do? Is it too late to change his mind once he has called a play in the huddle?

No. If a quarterback thinks that the play he already called will be a disaster, since the defense may have already figured out what he intends to do, he can change the play at the line of scrimmage. He can call an **audible**, in which he yells a new, different series of codes and numbers and chooses a new cadence.

You can see how important it is for each player to know every play code and to listen carefully to everything the quarterback says. You can also imagine just how frustrating and difficult it can be for some players, especially the wide receivers who line up farthest away from the quarterback, to hear clearly when the crowd is making a lot of noise. At times, you will see that the quarterback and/or his teammates are having difficulty communicating with one another other due to the deafening noise in a stadium. This noise is usually generated by the defensive team's home fans who want to distract the quarterback and his teammates as much as possible, so that they may become confused and misrun the play. Sometimes there is so much noise, you will see the quarterback noticeably turn his head and yell louder or call a time out because he knows that his teammates cannot hear him.

If the noise continues to a point where the quarterback is unable to start a new play after making several attempts, the officials may get involved. If the officials determine that the defense's home fans are causing too much of a disturbance with their noise that results in a disruption or delay of the game, then they can assess a penalty to the defensive team. Since the defense is always aware of the possibility of receiving a "noise" penalty, at times you will see team members gesturing to the crowd to lower the noise level.

Line of Scrimmage

The **line of scrimmage** is an imaginary line that runs the width of the field and through the tip of the football. Both the offense and the defense have their respective lines of scrimmage nearest to their own goal lines. The area between the two tips of the football or the two lines of scrimmage is called the **neutral zone**. It extends to the point to which the offensive team has advanced. The two teams face each other on their lines of scrimmage before each play begins.

For example, if you are watching or listening to a game and hear the announcer say, "The Eagles have the ball on the 34-yard line," or "It's first down and 10 from

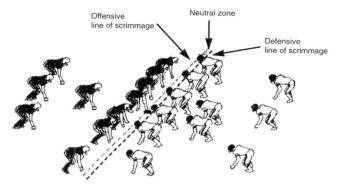

4.8 LINE OF SCRIMMAGE

the 34-yard line," the 34-yard line is the line of scrimmage, the point from which the play begins.

The exact line of scrimmage is very important to the quarterback. He cannot throw a forward pass from beyond the line of scrimmage.

You may also hear the term **territory** being used in a football game. Territory, when used to describe a war, is the land which a country occupies and defends. The football analogy is similar: a team's territory is the part of the playing field that it defends. That is why the end of the field that a particular team is defending (i.e., has behind it) is called its **own end**, and the goal line is referred to as the team's **own goal line**.

Advancing the Ball

The team with the ball (offense) needs to advance the ball 10 yards in four tries or will have to relinquish it to the other team. If the team gets 10 or more yards on the first try, it's a first down.

When a team first gets possession of the ball, one of the following things may occur:

1. It may continue to pick up **first downs** by gaining at least 10 yards in 4 or fewer plays until it crosses its opponent's goal line for a touchdown.

2. It fails to gain the necessary 10 yards for a first down and must give the ball to its opponent **on downs** and the direction of the previous play is then reversed. In other words, the defense becomes the offense and begins play going in the opposite direction from the place where the previous play ended. The players will change units on the field.

3. It fails to gain 10 yards within 4 or fewer plays and attempts to kick a field goal.

4. It fails to gain 10 yards within 4 or fewer plays and punts (kicks) the ball to its opponent.

5. It loses the ball to the defense through an error such as an interception or a fumble.

Offense

You already know that the **offense** is the unit that has the ball. You know that the quarterback is a member and leader of that unit, but can you recall the other members of the offense? The offensive unit usually consists of two **wide receivers (WR)**, one **tight end (TE)**, two **tackles (T)**, two **guards (G)**, one **center (C)**, one **quarterback (QB)**, and two **running backs (RB)**.

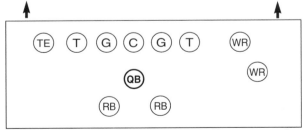

QB- Quarterback, C-Center, TE-Tight End, G-Guard, T-Tackle, RB-Running Back, WR-Wide Receiver

4.9 OFFENSE

The offense must have at least seven players on the line of scrimmage and the backfield players must be at least one yard behind the line of scrimmage. The primary responsibility of some of these players is blocking, of which there are two basic types. In **run blocking**, the ball is snapped and the blockers push their opponents away from the ball carrier. Sometimes you might see quick run blockers on a team such as a tight end or a running back. They provide the lead block and clear a path for the ball carrier, who is following behind. **Pass blocking** is done on a passing play. The lineman and backs try to keep members of the defense from getting to their quarterback for as long as possible so he has a chance to throw and, hopefully, complete a pass.

Although there are numerous plays that the offense can use to move the ball, all plays not involving a kick fall into two basic categories: **running** and **passing**.

Running

During a **running play** (a play in which a player runs with the ball), the back who receives the ball tries either to advance across the line of scrimmage by running straight ahead (**up the middle**), to the outside of his tackles (**off-tackle**), or around either end of the line. To accomplish these tasks, his offensive linemen must **run interference** for him (**block** – that is, keep the opposing team's players away). Any player who runs with the ball is known as the **ball carrier**. A ball handed to the runner is called a **handoff**.

Passing

During a **passing play** (a play in which one player throws the ball to one of his teammates), a **forward pass** is thrown by a back, usually the quarterback, from *behind* the line of scrimmage to an eligible receiver downfield. If the pass is caught (**completed**), the receiver continues to run toward his opponent's goal line until he is tackled, goes out of bounds, or crosses the goal line for a touchdown. If the pass is not caught for any reason (**incomplete**), the ball is then returned to the line of scrimmage. Only one forward pass is permitted on each play, and only backs and ends are eligible receivers.

Defense

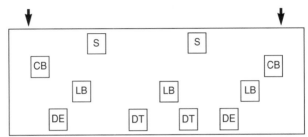

DT-Defensive Tackle, DE-Defensive End, LB-Linebacker, S-Safety, CB-Cornerback

4.10 DEFENSE

What about the defense? The 11-member defense usually has two **ends (DE)**, two **tackles (DT)**, three **linebackers (LB)** and four **defensive backs (DB)** comprised of two **cornerbacks** and two **safeties**. Like the offense, the defense can choose dozens of defensive alignments depending upon the particular situation in which it finds itself or in response to the formation of the offense. Diagram 4.10 shows a basic defensive alignment.

The rules of football allow the alignments of the defensive team to be more flexible than offensive formations. Usual defensive alignments call for four to six linemen to face the opposing team at the line of scrimmage. The rest of the defensive unit is behind them. Two to four linebackers are usually directly behind the defensive linemen. Three or four defensive backs, who make up the secondary, position themselves about 10 yards beyond the line of scrimmage.

Different situations call for the offense to use certain types of play. The defense tries to guess what type of play the offense will use and then sets up an alignment to guard against it. For example, when the defense expects a running play, the defensive backs become less important and you see more players being used in or close to the line of scrimmage. If, on the other hand, the defense expects a passing play, you see fewer linemen in the formation and more players playing pass defense.

In the Trenches: Offense vs. Defense

The **trenches** or the **pits** refers to the area where the interior linemen meet the defensive linemen at the line of scrimmage. It is in the trenches where you will see a lot of interaction as the defense tries to prevent the offense from moving the ball.

The Snap

After the offense comes out of the huddle, it lines up opposite the defense on the line of scrimmage. Most players line up in a **three-point stance**, one in which players lean forward and place one hand (and two feet, thus the three points!) on the ground preparing themselves to charge forward when the ball is snapped. The center (C) of the offensive team, also called the **snapper**, crouches over the football and begins the play. When he hears a particular signal

4.11 THE CENTER SNAP

(also called the cadence or count) from the quarterback, the center **snaps** or **hikes** the ball; that is, he passes or hands it back between his legs.

Most often the center hands the ball to the quarterback, who in turn can pass it, hand it off or run with it. However, sometimes the center may pass the ball directly to one of the backs other than the quarterback. The player who gets the ball may run with it, pass it laterally or forward, or kick it, as in the case of a field goal or punt. Keep in mind that any play consisting of either running or passing maneuvers ends when the ball carrier is tackled, forced out of bounds, or scores a touchdown.

Offensive players check defenders or try to force them out of the way by performing the maneuver known as **blocking**, one of the most fundamental skills in football. Players may block only with their bodies, not their hands or arms. The ball carrier, however, is allowed to use his arm to ward off or **straight arm/stiff arm** potential tacklers.

Defensive players may use their arms and hands in an attempt to break through the opponent's line to reach the ball carrier. The defense tries to keep its opponents from gaining yardage; in fact, it even tries to stop them for a *loss* of yardage by tackling the ball carrier before he even reaches the line of scrimmage.

Downs

One of the most confusing aspects of the game of football is the calculation of downs and yardage from play to play. Besides penalties, downs and yardage are the topics that need more review and practice than any other. They are not all that difficult if you take them step by step. It's helpful to know how to calculate downs and yardage yourself during a game,

4.12 FIRST DOWN

53

although the announcers and the stadium scoreboard provide this information.

The offense has four chances or **downs** to gain 10 yards. If it can gain 10 yards in four or fewer plays, it gets a new first down and can keep possession of the football. However, if it fails to gain the 10 yards necessary for a first down in four or fewer plays, it must give up the ball to its opponent. It's as simple as that.

The number to remember whenever a team first gets the ball or gets a first down is 10, meaning 10 yards to go. The first play, therefore, is **first down and 10**; that is, the first play with 10 yards to gain for a new first down. What is the next down after the first down play has been completed? How do you figure it out?

Step 1:   **Add one down to the previous down.**

This is done except in cases where the team gained at least 10 yards for a new first down or when there is a penalty. For example, a team has a first down and 10 and runs a play. If the team can gain at least 10 yards on the play, it's first down and 10 again. But what happens if a team can't gain the 10 yards necessary for a new first down? It becomes second down, but second down and how many yards to go?

How does the yardage figure in?

Step 2:   **Subtract the yards gained on the new play from the previous yardage to go.**

Step 3:   **Combine the down and the yardage.**

Suppose your team has a first down and 10, runs a play and gains 5 yards. How do you describe the next play?

Since the team did not gain 10 yards, it is not a new first down. So you added one to the previous down (first down), and it now becomes second down. But second down and how may yards to go?

To calculate the yardage to go for succeeding plays, always subtract the amount gained from the previous yardage to go. Remember, it was first and 10 yards to go. In our example, the team gained 5 yards, so subtract that 5 yards from 10 yards and you get 5 yards still to go. Therefore, the correct way to describe the next play is second down and 5 yards to go, or more commonly, second and 5.

Let's try another example to make sure you understand this down concept. Suppose the Washington Redskins have a third down and 7 yards (third and 7) to go, and gain 6 yards. How is the next play announced?

Step 1:   **Add one down to the previous down (third down + 1 = fourth down)**

Step 2:   **Subtract the amount gained from the previous yardage. Remember that the previous yardage was 7. (7 yards minus 6 yards gained = 1 yard.)**

Step 3:   **Combine the down and the yardage. (fourth down and 1)**

Your answer should be fourth down and 1.

Loss of Yardage

What if the team *loses* yardage instead of gains? Suppose, for example, the New England Patriots have a second down and 4 yards to go. Their opponents, the Green Bay Packers, anticipate New England's play and tackle the ball carrier for a loss of 5 yards. How do you describe the next play?

Step 1:   **Add one to the previous down (second + 1 = third down)**

Step 2:   **Add the amount of loss to the previous yardage. The amount of the loss is 5 yards and the previous yardage was 4. (5 yards + 4 yards = 9 yards)**

Step 3:   **Combine the down and the yards. (third down and 9)**

Down and Goal

How would you describe the down situation in the following example? The Seattle Seahawks have been advancing the ball down the field and get a first down on the San Diego Chargers' 6-yard line. Yes, it's a first down, but is it first and 10? No. Why not?

In cases like this, it is not first down and 10 because the offensive team is within its opponent's 10-yard line. In other words, the offense would cross the goal line before it gained 10 yards, the amount needed for a first down. What do we do when the team is on the 6-yard line and has a first down?

The proper term to use here is **first down and goal**. The term **"and goal"** is used whenever the offense has fewer than 10 yards to go for a touchdown. In the above example involving the Seahawks, you would describe the play as **first down and goal from the 6**. The succeeding downs are calculated using the same formula by adding one down to the previous down, just as if 10 yards were involved, but instead of stating the yardage needed, you should always use "and goal."

Chain Crew/Gang

Periodically, a group of uniformed men comes onto the field with a 10-yard chain to assist the officiating crew in measuring the distance needed for first downs. Keep your eye on them; they are known as the **chain crew or gang**. The referee will measure the ball with the chain; if the offense *has not* made a first down, he will indicate with his hands the amount of yardage still needed. If a first down *has* been made, he points in the direction of the defensive team's goal line, or, in other words, in the scoring direction of the offense.

Fourth Down Options

If a team is able to continuously pick up first downs and advance the ball down the field, it will cross its opponent's goal line for a touchdown. If the offense fails to gain the necessary 10 yards for a first down in three plays, it then becomes fourth down, the last chance to gain the remaining yardage. What does a team do when it is faced with a fourth down situation?

It has several options from which to choose:

- Try to gain the yardage necessary for the first down
- Attempt to kick a field goal
- Punt the ball to its opponent

Let's take a look at what's involved with each of these options. Always remember that the first thing a team considers on fourth down is its field position. We'll use an example involving the New York Jets and the Minnesota Vikings to illustrate fourth down options. The Jets have the ball on their own 35-yard line and are faced with a fourth down and 2 yards to go. What should they do?

1. **Try to gain the yardage necessary for a first down** (in football language, this is called **"going for it"**).

Two yards is really not a lot of yardage to gain, but if New York does not gain 2 yards, it must turn the ball over to the Vikings at the spot where the fourth down play ends. This will result in Minnesota's having the ball deep within the Jets' territory and relatively close to the Jets' goal line (only 35 yards away). This would provide the Vikings with an excellent position on the field and a relatively easy scoring opportunity.

2. **Attempt to kick a field goal**.

On fourth down situations, teams may choose to attempt a field goal by placekicking the ball over the crossbar of its opponent's goal post. If you were New

York's head coach and your team were on its own 35-yard line, would you attempt a field goal? Yes or no? Why or why not? Let's see what's involved in deciding whether or not to attempt a field goal.

Calculating the distance of a field goal

When calculating the distance of a field goal, the coach must first figure out the distance between the line of scrimmage (the spot where the ball is) and the opponent's goal line. If his team is in its own territory, he thinks of the playing field as having 100 yards. He subtracts the yard line where the ball is from 100 yards.

If the Buffalo Bills, for example, had the ball on their own 42-yard line, the coach would subtract 42 from 100, equaling a distance of 58 yards between the line of scrimmage and the opponent's goal line.

If the team is within its opponent's territory, whatever yard line the ball is on will tell you the distance to the opponent's goal line. For example, if the Pittsburgh Steelers were on the New Orleans Saints' 29-yard line, 29 yards would be the distance between the line of scrimmage and the opponent's goal line.

Let's get back to our case involving the New York Jets with a fourth down and 2 on their own 35-yard line. How would the coach calculate the field goal distance? Since his team is within its own territory, he would subtract the line of scrimmage (35) from 100 yards. (100 yards minus 35 yards = 65 yards). The coach calculates the distance between the line of scrimmage and the opponent's goal line as being 65 yards. He then adds 17 yards to that distance.

17 yards? Why 17 yards?

The kicker must kick the ball from a position 7 yards *behind* the line of scrimmage making for 7 extra yards. You must also consider the fact that the goal post is 10 yards beyond the goal line, making for 10 additional yards. So, whenever you are calculating the distance of a field goal, add 17 yards to the total distance between the line of scrimmage and the opponent's goal line. In our case, the distance was 65 yards between the New York 35-yard line and the Minnesota goal line. With 17 yards added, it would make for an 82-yard field goal attempt for the Jets.

Although placekickers in the National Football League are skilled athletes who are accurate in kicking field goals, New York would have to have Superman kicking the ball to have any chance whatsoever of making an 82-yard field goal. Since the Minnesota goal line is not within the range of New York's place kicker, the head coach decides not to attempt a field goal.

There is only one more option for the Jets to consider:

3. Punt (or kick) to the opposing team.

In football jargon, this is sometimes called **"three and out,"** meaning the offense runs three plays, does not gain 10 yards and must go out of the game and the punting team comes in. Some people also refer to this as the **"Rockettes' Offense"** (1, 2, 3 kick!).

Since the Jets have eliminated the options of attempting to gain the necessary 2 yards and attempting a field goal, the only other viable option is to punt the football. A punt will force the Vikings to start play at the other end of the field, deep in their own territory. After the receiving team of the Vikings takes possession of the ball, its offensive unit takes the field and tries to advance the ball against the New York defense.

You will see these options in every game: the more conservative teams tend to punt the ball more often on fourth down, whereas the risk takers in the NFL often try to gain the yardage ("go for it") or attempt longer-than-average field goals. You will notice more risky behavior occurring late in the game when the offense is behind and must absolutely keep the ball in a last ditch attempt to score points and win the game.

Turnovers

During a football game, possession of the ball changes back and forth from team to team. Sometimes the offense may give up (turn over) the football to the defense by making an error. These errors are called **turnovers** and fall into two categories: **interceptions** and **fumbles**.

Interception

An interception occurs when any defensive player catches a forward pass that was intended for an offensive player. If he catches the ball before it hits the ground, he makes an interception and begins to run in the direction opposite the way the offense was heading. He then becomes an offensive player and tries to advance the ball as far as he can before being tackled or going out of bounds. Once he is tackled, his offensive unit comes out onto the field, takes over possession of the ball, then tries to advance the ball and score.

Fumble

A fumble is defined as an act when a player loses possession of the ball, that is, drops or otherwise mishandles it except when he passes, kicks, or hands the ball off. Whenever my father would see a fumble, he would say laughingly, "Don't go near a loose ball, it attracts crowds!" Actually, only the latter part of that statement is true in football. Fumbles definitely draw a lot of attention, but football players *never* try to avoid a loose ball. You will see players diving all over the place trying to recover a loose ball; in fact, there may be a group of players in a pile on the ground all fighting for possession.

If there are several players fighting for control of the ball, how do you know which team has recovered? Watch the referee. He will go to the pile of players and make his decision after the players get off one another. Once he sees who has the football, he indicates possession by pointing his arm in the scoring direction of the recovering team, or, in other words, towards the goal line of the team that *didn't* recover the fumble. A fumble is not considered to be a turnover unless the team that fumbles it loses possession.

Turnovers tell you a lot about how well a team is playing. The more turnovers a team has, the less likely it is that it will win the game. As you learn more about football, you will come to appreciate the importance of turnovers, especially when they occur deep in the offensive team's territory. You often hear announcers or sportswriters say that turnovers cost a team a win.

Although some of the formations, strategies and NFL rules can be somewhat confusing, the game itself is actually not all that difficult to learn. Just keep this book handy, watch your television screen, and listen to your announcers. The play-by-play procedures will begin to make sense in no time at all!

☑ CHAPTER 4 CHECKLIST
THINGS TO REMEMBER

- **Offense**
  2 wide receivers (WR)
  1 tight end (TE)
  2 tackles (T)
  2 guards (G)
  1 center (C)
  1 quarterback (QB)
  2 running backs (RB)
  11 total

  Defense
  2 ends (DE)
  2 tackles (DT)
  3 linebackers (LB)
  4 defensive backs (DB)
  11 total

- Four downs to gain 10 yards
- Rules to calculate downs (if there is no penalty or a gain of 10 yards on the previous play)
- Add one down to the previous down.
- If the team gained yards, subtract the yards from the previous yardage.
- If the team lost yardage, add the yards lost to the previous yardage.
- If a team has fewer than 10 yards to go for a touchdown, use the term "and goal" instead of the number of yards to go.
- To calculate field goal distance:
  1. Figure out the distance between the line of scrimmage and the opponent's goal line.
  2. Add 17 yards to that figure.

TERMS TO KNOW

blocking	huddle	neutral zone
coin toss	interception	sudden death
down	line of scrimmage	turnover
fumble		

EXTRA POINTS: DID YOU KNOW?

The record for the longest field goal was set by Tom Dempsey of the New Orleans Saints. Dempsey, who was born with no toes on his right foot and with a right arm that ended in only two fingers without a hand, booted himself into the NFL record books on November 8, 1970. Dempsey kicked the record 63-yarder with only 2 seconds left in the game to give his team a thrilling 19-17 victory over the Detroit Lions.

CHAPTER 5

TIMING

"Make it stop...Please make it stop!"
- Debbie Francescott (1994)

There is some confusion among football novices regarding the length of a football game. If a football game has only one hour of playing time, why does it take an average of three or more hours to complete? For novice football spectators, this might seem like an eternity! Games can also seem longer if your team is being blown out of the water by its opponent. The above quote, for example, was made while viewing a seemingly endless game in which the San Francisco 49ers solidly beat New York Giants with a score of 44-3.

The actual playing time in a football game is 60 minutes. The game is divided into halves, each consisting of two **periods** called **quarters.** The intermission between the halves, called **halftime**, lasts 12 minutes unless otherwise specified. There are also two-minute rest periods after the first and third quarters.

How do the officials keep time in a football game?

The Clock

During a football game, one or two clocks appear on your television screen or on the scoreboard. One is the official or game clock and the other is the play or second clock, also sometimes referred to as the 40/25 clock. What is the difference between the two?

The **official clock** displays the amount of time left in a specific quarter of the game. The clock is set at 15:00 at the beginning of each quarter and winds down until the end of the quarter when the clock reads 00:00. It is at this time that the line judge fires a starter pistol to indicate that the time in the quarter has expired and it is time for the teams to switch goals. This happens at the end of the first and third quarters.

The **play clock** displays the number of seconds that the offense has to start a play. Time between plays cannot be any longer than 40 seconds. This 40 seconds refers to the time from the end of a given play until the snap of the ball for the next play. There are also times when there is a 25-second interval (thus the name 40/25 second clock) after certain administrative stoppages and game delays. If the play clock runs out and the team has not started a new play, it is penalized 5 yards for **delay of game**.

When the ball is not in play, the play clock is always stopped. When do the officials stop the official clock?

Time outs

The official clock is stopped in these instances:

- Following a touchdown, field goal, 2-point conversion, or safety
- During an extra point attempt after a touchdown
- When the ball or a ball carrier goes out of bounds
- When a receiver makes a fair catch
- After incomplete passes
- When penalties are being assessed

- At the end of the first and third periods when the teams change goals
- At the **two minute warning** – The official signals there are two minutes remaining to play in the first half or in the game
- Following a change in possession
- During first down measurements
- At the end of a down after a foul occurs
- After throwing a pass out of bounds or intentionally spiking the ball
- For technical reasons – i.e., television commercials
- Because of player injury (two minutes)
- For equipment repair (three minutes)

In addition to these official time outs, each team is allowed three time outs (one minute and 50 seconds each) per half except during the final two minutes of the half when the team is allowed only 40 seconds for its time outs. Consecutive team time outs can be taken by opposing teams, but the second time out can be a maximum of only 40 seconds.

5.1 TIME OUT

Sudden Death

When the score is tied at the end of the regulation playing time in an NFL game, the teams continue to play in an overtime period using the system called **sudden death**. A sudden death overtime period of 15 minutes begins after a three-minute intermission at the end of the regulation game. The team that first scores a touchdown, field goal or safety during this overtime period is the winner, and the game automatically ends with that score. As with a regulation game, the overtime period begins with the usual pre-game coin toss. The captain of the visiting team calls the toss.

During pre-season and regular season games, only one 15-minute sudden death overtime period is played. If neither team scores, then the game ends in a tie. In post-season play-off games, however, teams continue to play 15 minute overtime periods (with two time outs permitted) until there is a score. Although the overtime period is technically a new quarter, those players who might have been ejected during the regulation game are not allowed to return.

This brief explanation should help eliminate some of the confusion surrounding the length of a football game. When the clock is stopped during a game, try to figure out the specific reason why it was stopped. Was it a penalty? Injury? Referee's time out? Television commercial? With so many reasons to call a time out, it is no wonder a Sunday during football season may seem to some to be the longest day of the week!

CHAPTER 5 CHECKLIST
THINGS TO REMEMBER

- 60 minutes of playing time per game, with one 12-minute halftime.
- Four quarters/periods of 15 minutes each per game.
- Three time outs per team per half.

TERMS TO KNOW

delay of game
game clock
official clock
second/play clock

sudden death overtime
time out
two minute warning

EXTRA POINTS: DID YOU KNOW?

The record for the longest NFL game (eighty-two minutes and forty seconds) ever played was set on December 25, 1971. It was an AFC Divisional playoff game between the Miami Dolphins and the Kansas City Chiefs. This game went into double sudden death overtime. Finally, halfway through the sixth quarter, the Miami Dolphins won 27-24 with a 37-yard field goal.

CHAPTER 6

OFFENSE

"What do the players talk about when they cuddle together on the field?" - Laurie W. (1992)

As you know by now, during each play teams are designated as either the **offensive team**, that is, the team in possession of the ball – or the **defensive team**, the team defending its goal line.

This chapter takes a look at how the offense lines up at its line of scrimmage. To the untrained eye, it may appear as if football players line up the same way play after play, but this is not the case. Both the offense and defense have dozens of formations to use when positioning themselves at the line of scrimmage. This chapter describes and illustrates different **offensive formations**, strategies and plays to watch for when viewing a game.

When watching a game, try not to make the most common spectator mistake, that of concentrating almost exclusively on the location of the football. Although it is helpful to know where the ball is, you can learn a great deal by scanning the entire field, either in the stadium itself or on your television screen. Try to train yourself to look at the field and not at the ball before the snap. As the play unfolds, you will be able to find the ball by watching the interaction of the offense and defense.

So, if you don't look for the ball, what should you be doing?

You should try to figure out what formation (**set**) the offense is using. That's easier said than done! These next few diagrams will help you identify the most common NFL formations.

FORMATIONS

Pro Set

This is an offensive formation that includes a quarterback, two running backs, two wide receivers, a tight end, and five middle linemen.

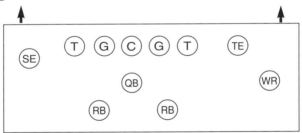

QB- Quarterback, C-Center, TE-Tight End, G-Guard, T-Tackle, RB-Running Back, SE-Split End, WR-Wide Receiver/Flanker

6.1 PRO SET

The **pro set** is the most common formation in professional football and has been the basic formation in the NFL for almost 30 years. This formation has several advantages:

• It makes a passing play a constant threat to the defense because it has a wide receiver out to each side.

- It can provide for balanced running plays: a running back can run either straight ahead or **off-tackle**, that is, run to the outside of his offensive tackle.

Shotgun Set

The **shotgun set** is the formation in which the quarterback takes the snap at least 5 yards behind the center instead of directly behind him. In the shotgun formation, the ball is **shot** back to the quarterback like a bullet out of a gun instead of being directly handed to him. When you see a shotgun formation, it is a good indication that the offense is going to pass the ball. The shotgun formation has several advantages:

- Since defensive players rush in as soon as the ball is snapped, the shotgun set gives the quarterback a few more seconds to throw the ball.

- It gives the quarterback a little more time to spot his receivers downfield.

- By the time the quarterback is ready to pass the ball, his receivers will have had time to get open downfield.

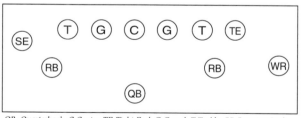

QB- Quarterback, C-Center, TE-Tight End, G-Guard, T-Tackle, RB-Running Back, SE-Split End, WR-Wide Receiver/Flanker

6.2 Shotgun Set

I Formation

The **I formation** is the formation in which the running backs line up directly behind the quarterback. As you might have already guessed, the I formation is the ideal formation to use if the team wants to run with the ball. This formation has the quarterback and the two running backs, the **fullback** and the **tailback**, lining up in the shape of the letter I.

The I formation gives the running back plenty of time to assess the situation in front of him, because he sets up deep behind the quarterback. He is able to look at his offensive line as well as the defensive alignment and wait for a hole in the line to appear before he starts his run. This formation is particularly effective for running plays through the middle of the line or off-tackle.

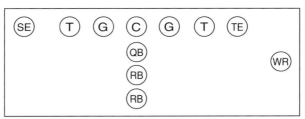

QB- Quarterback, C-Center, TE-Tight End, G-Guard, T-Tackle, RB-Running Back, SE-Split End, WR-Wide Receiver/Flanker

6.3 I Formation

Short Yardage Formation

As the name suggests, the **short yardage formation** is used when there are only a couple of yards to go to the goal line or to make a first down. Most of these offenses

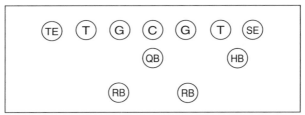

QB- Quarterback, C-Center, TE-Tight End, G-Guard, T-Tackle, RB-Running Back, SE-Split End, HB-Halfback

6.4 Short Yardage Formation

bring in an extra tight end to replace a wide receiver, who plugs up a hole on the weak side and makes the formation strong on both sides.

Down and Distance

If you can't identify the offensive formation in front of you, how else can you get a general sense of what type of play the offense may use? You become familiar with the general rule that coaches refer to as **down and distance**. How does the down and distance rule work?

First you must know what the **down** is and how many yards are needed to get to a new first down, or the **distance**. Once you know those two pieces of information, you can use down and distance.

First Down

On a first down play, you can expect either a running or a passing play. Although at the beginning of the game many teams frequently run on first down, they tend to use combinations of runs and passes as the game progresses. Teams want to make good yardage, that is, at least four or five yards on first down plays. If they are successful on first downs, then there will be fewer yards to gain on later downs.

Second Down and Long Yardage or Third Down and Long Yardage

When five or more yards are needed for a first down, second and third down plays are usually passing downs. For these types of plays, you will see teams use more wide receivers and running backs who are also good pass receivers. To prepare for a passing situation, the defensive team usually substitutes more defensive backs for linebackers and defensive linemen.

Second Down and Four Yards To Go

On this play, expect the offense to call either a run or a pass.

Second Down and Short Yardage

Second down and short yardage is a time when coaches often call for a big play such as a long pass. Even if the big play doesn't work, the offense can still make the yardage necessary for the first down on the next play, the third down.

Third Down and Short Yardage

This play is usually a running play when only a couple of yards are needed to make a first down. Offenses usually use two or three tight ends, fewer wide receivers and larger running backs. In anticipation of this running play, the defense takes out its defensive backs and puts in more defensive linemen.

OFFENSIVE PLAYS

Now that we have reviewed common formations and game strategies, let's take a look at several types of commonly used offensive plays. Remember that the idea behind all offensive plays is for the **offensive linemen** to ward off attacking defenders by blocking. They either make a hole in the line for the running back to pass through or they move to protect the quarterback, giving him ample time to complete a pass.

It is important to realize just how vital offensive linemen are on a football team. Although these players generally do not receive nearly as much media attention as others, their teammates, particularly running backs and quarterbacks, fully appreciate the critical role they play and have shown their appreciation to their linemen in various ways. For example, Troy Aikman, quarterback for the Dallas Cowboys, reportedly bought his linemen handmade cowboy boots and airline tickets to anywhere in the world. Buffalo Bill running back Thurman Thomas has honored his linemen with engraved crystal bison statues, while his counterpart on the Dallas Cowboys, Emmitt Smith, has presented Rolex watches to his linemen, and champagne to *all* members of the team.

All offensive plays fall into three categories: **running** (also known as **rushing**), **passing** and **kicking**. The football can be kicked or passed only from behind the line of scrimmage. Any time the offense crosses over its line of scrimmage with the ball, it must carry out a running play.

6.5 BALL CARRIER

RUNNING PLAYS

Although there are many different running plays that are used in football, here are the ones you see most often.

Sweep   A running play in which the ball carrier takes a handoff from the quarterback and runs parallel to the line of scrimmage. He allows his blockers, made up of the guards and sometimes a tackle, to get in front of him as his protection, then turns or **sweeps** the corner around one of the ends of the line of scrimmage.

Dive   The **dive** involves the running back taking a quick handoff from the quarterback and running through the hole between his offensive tackle and guard. Often another running back is also out in front of the ball carrier. This play is used most often for **short yardage** situations, that is, when the offense needs less than a yard to make a first down or a touchdown.

Pitch	During a **pitch** or **pitchout**, the quarterback tosses a short **lateral** (an underhand toss made behind or parallel to the line of scrimmage) to a running back.
Trap	This play can be considered either one of the most spectacular running plays or one of football's best "sucker" plays, depending upon your point of view. During this play, one of the middle linemen (the center, tackle, or guard), leaves his normal blocking area and moves away to one side, allowing a defensive lineman to penetrate the offensive line. Because he is not being blocked, the charger is faked into believing he has a clear shot into the backfield area. Instead, as he is going through the hole, he is blocked out by an offensive linemen from the opposite side.
Draw Play	The offense uses the draw play as another "fake" play. In order to fool the opposition, the team gives the impression that the play will involve a pass, when it is actually a running play. The quarterback drops back almost to his normal passing position and the offensive linemen block as if they were providing him pass protection. But instead of passing the ball, the quarterback hands the ball off to a running back. In this play, the defense is **"drawn"** into thinking a pass is coming, when the simulated pass play actually turns into a run.
Quarterback Sneak	Like the dive, this play is an excellent choice for short yardage situations. When only a yard or less is needed for a first down or a touchdown, the offense may use a play known as the **quarterback sneak**. In this play, the quarterback takes

	the snap from the center and runs straight ahead through the line behind the blocking of his center and guards.
Bootleg	To carry out the **bootleg**, another short yardage play, the quarterback fakes a handoff to one of his running backs, hides the ball against his hip/leg and runs in the direction opposite to the fake handoff. Nowadays, the bootleg play is not used as often as in the past because coaches are reluctant to have their high-salaried quarterbacks risk injury by running with the football.
Slant	During a **slant** play, the running back runs at an angle or slant toward the hole in the line. The other running back in the lineup also runs at that same angle to lead the blocking interference.
Reverse	A **reverse** is a fun play to watch. The quarterback hands off to a running back who runs toward the sideline. The running back, in turn, hands the ball off to a teammate who is going in the opposite direction in the backfield.

6.6 PASSER

PASSING PLAYS

If an offensive play does not involve kicking or is not a running play, it is a **passing play.** As with running plays, there are numerous plays involving a forward pass. Receivers are generally the quickest players on a football team; they must be able to run accurate pass patterns, and have "good hands" to enable them to catch all types of passes.

Pass Patterns

When the offense is in the huddle, the quarterback calls the next play that the team will run. If it is a passing play, the quarterback needs to inform every receiver of three things:

- Where he should line up (formation)
- The snap count (when the ball will be snapped)
- The pass pattern (route he should run)

The quarterback uses a series of numbers or the cadence to convey this information so that all of the players, not just the receivers, know what pass pattern is being used. Some teams use two or three digit codes to describe the pass patterns of all their receivers.

A **pass pattern** or **pass route** is a set of maneuvers executed by a receiver as he prepares to catch a pass. Most teams develop their passing game around a basic set of common pass patterns.

Although you may see receivers run different pass patterns during a game, there are some that are used more often than others. What kinds of pass patterns do receivers run? What do they look like? Good questions. The answers to these questions can be found by looking at a **passing tree**.

A passing tree?

A **passing tree** is a diagram that, when drawn on a blackboard, looks very much like a leafless tree. The branches on the tree represent the various pass routes a receiver can run. Since wide receivers, tight ends, and running backs are all eligible receivers, teams have separate passing trees for each group.

The following diagram shows a passing tree for wide receivers, who use speed and quick moves with their heads and bodies to shake off their defender(s) to **"get open,"** that is, to be in a position to catch a pass.

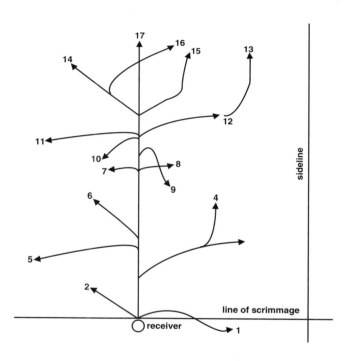

1. screen	7. hook in	13. out and fly
2. slant	8. hook out	14. post
3. short out	9. comeback	15. fly
4. short out and up	10. curl	16. corner
5. cross	11. in	17. up
6. quick post	12. out	

6.7 PASSING TREE

Below are some of the most common pass patterns. (Refer to Diagram 6.7 for help!)

Out   On an **out** pattern, the receiver runs and then makes a quick break to the sidelines at an angle, coming back toward the line of scrimmage. This action prevents the pass defender from getting to the ball.

Curl   The receiver runs downfield and makes a quick turn back toward the line of scrimmage to catch the ball.

Fly   This is a long pass pattern in which the wide receiver runs straight ahead downfield at full speed.

Slant   This pattern involves the receiver leaving the line of scrimmage, taking two or three steps, then running across the middle of the field at approximately a 45-degree angle.

Post   A **post** pattern involves the receiver breaking to his defender's inside shoulder to get the defender to turn the wrong way. Then, the receiver cuts upfield toward the goal line.

Fade   The receiver takes two or three steps from the line of scrimmage, then runs towards the sidelines at approximately a 45-degree angle. You will see this frequently used when the offense is inside the opponent's 20-yard line and the quarterback throws to his receiver in the corner of the end zone. *(not shown in Diagram 6.7)*

There are many types of pass patterns that can be used by wide receivers, tight ends, and running backs. Watching the receivers run certain routes is a good way for you to learn more about the passing game. By watching their routes, those defenders who are doing the best jobs of providing solid pass coverage can be identified.

Keep in mind that when a quarterback throws a forward pass, he may not necessarily be throwing to the receiver, but rather to the location at the end of the receiver's pass pattern. Sometimes you will see a quarterback overthrow, underthrow, completely miss his receiver, or throw the ball to a spot where his receiver "isn't." Although it may look to the contrary, this may not be the quarterback's fault; it may be the fault of the receiver. Several things may come into play: field and weather conditions may hinder the running of the pass pattern; the defender interferes with the receiver; or the receiver may run the wrong pattern.

A team's passing game can be one of the most spectacular aspects of its entire strategy. Championship caliber teams try to develop a balanced offense that includes both a good running/rushing game and a passing attack involving the entire field and using a combination of short, medium and long distance passes. The following are the most common passing plays.

Play Action

This play, involving the quarterback and his running back, has been used to confuse many defensive teams over the years. The idea of **play action** is to make the play look exactly like a run when it is actually a pass. The quarterback fakes a handoff to the running back who then pretends to take the ball and runs downfield. The defense makes the running back its target, because they think that the running back is the one carrying the ball. The quarterback, meanwhile, drops back and throws to either his other running back or to one of his receivers.

During play action, in a split second the defensive players must decide if a running play or a passing play is coming at them. That split second decision often means the difference between the defense preventing the fake from taking place or the offense executing a successful play.

Screen Pass

This play fakes the defense into a false sense of security. The **screen pass** is used when the defense is expecting a running play. The offensive linemen allow members of the defense to penetrate into the offensive backfield. As this is happening, the offense sets up a blocking wall called the **pocket**. Then the quarterback flips a short pass to an eligible receiver positioned behind this blocking wall.

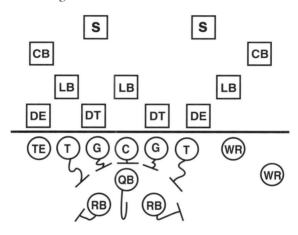

QB- Quarterback, C-Center, TE-Tight End, G-Guard, T-Tackle, RB-Running Back, DE-Defensive End, DT-Defensive Tackle, LB-Linebacker, CB-Cornerback, S-Safety

6.8 POCKET

Option Play

An **option play** involves an offensive player running with the ball behind the line of scrimmage, attempting to pass to a receiver. If he cannot find a receiver, he has the option of keeping the ball himself and running to pick up some yardage. There are either **quarterback options** or **halfback options**, with each player having the choice of running or passing.

Rollout

During this play, while remaining behind the line of scrimmage, the quarterback **"rolls out"** or runs out of the pocket in the direction of one of the sidelines. Since most quarterbacks are right handed, quarterbacks most often roll to their right. After the rollout, the quarterback throws a pass to one of his receivers.

The Bomb

The **bomb**, which is often considered as one of the most spectacular plays in football, is a term used to describe a long pass. When the quarterback is going to throw a bomb, he takes the ball either directly from the center, or if he is in a shotgun formation, from five or more yards back. He then throws the ball long to one of his receivers, who is attempting to get beyond the last defensive back downfield.

In some situations, such as at the end of the first half or at the end of the game, a team may attempt to throw a certain type of bomb called the **Hail Mary** pass. Roger Staubach, the Hall of Fame quarterback who played for the Dallas Cowboys, once described the Hail Mary pass as "one you throw up and pray that the receiver catches." The Hail Mary occurs when the quarterback throws a long, high pass into the opponent's end zone, hoping one of his receivers will catch it, or that one of the defenders will interfere with his receivers so that a penalty will be assessed and the offense will have possession of the ball near the opponent's goal line. This play is usually used in desperation when there is little time left on the clock; the offense has nothing to lose and makes a last ditch effort to put points on the scoreboard. As you probably have guessed, most Hail Mary passes are not completed; they are either intercepted, deflected, or fall incomplete. Nevertheless, they are exciting plays to watch.

The Flea Flicker

A **flea flicker** is a play designed to trick the defense into thinking a running play is about to occur. During a flea flicker, the quarterback hands the ball off to a running back who then pitches the ball back to the quarterback. The quarterback then throws a pass to one of his receivers. Of all the plays in professional football, I think the flea flicker is my personal favorite.

Keep an eye out for these plays, since they are the ones you will see most often. If you are watching a game on TV, pay attention to the announcers. You will hear them use these terms and may see them illustrate the actions and directions of the players on your television screen as well.

WHAT ELSE TO LOOK FOR

Now that you have become familiar with offensive formations and plays, let's discuss the specifics you should be looking for during a game. Having identified the type of formation being used, you have a valuable clue as to the nature of the next play.

You may wonder, "All this talk about formations is wonderful, but suppose I'm watching a game on television. I won't be able to see all of those positions on the screen."

Unfortunately, this is correct; the television cameras almost never show the entire offensive and defensive teams. Generally, only the offensive and defensive linemen, the offensive backfield, and occasionally the linebackers are visible. Unless you are actually at a game, you will rarely see the wide receivers or the defensive backs. Taking all that into account, how can you identify a play or keep track of the ball?

- Before each play, the football lies flat on the playing field between the two teams. Try to find the ball when the teams are in their huddles, and watch it as the teams break out of their huddles.

The center will walk directly to the ball, bend over and put his hands on it. The quarterback will be right behind him, bent over the center as the center gets ready to snap the ball between his legs.

- Before the snap of the ball, try to identify the offensive formation. How many running backs (jersey numbers 20-49), wide receivers (jersey numbers 80-89), and tight ends (jersey numbers 80-89 – lined up next to the offensive tackle) are lining up?

- Identify the number of players on the defensive line (jersey numbers 60-79, 90-99). Remember, the greater the number of players on the line, the greater the chance the defense is expecting a running play.

- If you can see any linebackers (jersey numbers 50-59, 90-99), ask yourself: Are they playing near the defensive linemen, indicating that they expect a running play? Are they playing deeper back, indicating they are looking for a passing play?

As soon as the ball is snapped, pay attention to the following:

- The quarterback – Watch the quarterback carefully to see what he does with the ball. Within two or three seconds after the snap of the ball, you should be able to tell if the play will be a running play or a passing play.

- The offensive linemen – Are they charging forward across the line of scrimmage? If they are, the play most likely is a run. Are they stepping back to form a pocket around the quarterback? If they are, then the play most likely involves a pass.

- The offensive blocking patterns – By watching the offensive blocking patterns, your eyes will eventually be led to the ball carrier on a running play or to the quarterback and, eventually, the receiver on a passing play.

The offensive team has a huge bag of tricks at its disposal for trying to advance the ball. You will come to prefer watching a game when teams use a mixture of plays involving runs, all types of passes, bombs, fakes, and gimmicks instead of relying on conservative (somewhat boring, in my estimation), repetitive forms of play.

If you follow these basic guidelines, you'll soon develop an increased understanding of the tactics and strategies of the game. By watching the pattern of offensive play and the defense's reactions to it, you may eventually be able to identify the best plays and strategies to use in particular situations.

CHAPTER 6 CHECKLIST
THINGS TO REMEMBER

- All offensive plays not involving a kick are either running plays or passing plays.

TERMS TO KNOW

bomb	pass patterns	rollout
bootleg	passing plays	running plays
dive	passing tree	screen
down and distance	pitch/pitch out	short yardage
draw	play action	shotgun
formations	pocket	sweep
Hail Mary	pro set	trap
I formation	quarterback sneak	

- When announcers refer to a "big" running play, it means a play which gains ten or more yards. When a "big" passing play takes place, it is one which involves a gain of 25 or more yards.

- Tony Dorsett, the former running back with the Dallas Cowboys and 1994 inductee into the Pro Football Hall of Fame, dashed into the NFL record books on January 3, 1983. It was on that day that Dorsett made the longest run from scrimmage (99 yards – the run started on his own 1 yard line) to score a touchdown against his opponents, the Minnesota Vikings.

- One of the greatest quarterbacks ever to play professional football was Joe Montana, who played from 1979 to 1992 with the San Francisco 49ers, and 1993 to 1994 with the Kansas City Chiefs. Although Montana retired in the spring of 1995, he still holds a wonderful reputation among NFL players and fans alike. A town in Montana has so much respect for him that it was renamed Joe, Montana.

CHAPTER 7

DEFENSE

"Isn't clipping a type of haircut?" - Abby F. (1993)

Because the defense has fewer line-up restrictions, it is more complicated than the offense. This chapter introduces the defense, basic defensive alignments, and the most common defensive plays in pro football.

The offensive unit in football gets most of the glamour and the glory, yet the defense and special teams must also perform well in order to ensure a win. It is general knowledge that the defense contributes a great deal to the overall success of a team. Games are often won due to the defense's fine performance. To a greater degree, a good defense can help a team win championships. Without a solid defense, a team cannot expect to have a winning record.

Although defensive formations called **alignments** can be very complicated, the motto of defense is actually very simple: *If your opponent does not score, your team cannot lose.* That makes sense, doesn't it? The underlying principle of great defense is: do not let the offense advance the ball on you, and try at every opportunity to get the football away from them. These defensive players look for a **turnover** on every play. (Remember that a turnover occurs when the offense gives up the ball to the defense through an error such as an interception or a fumble.)

In Chapter 6 you learned that different situations call for the use of certain offensive plays. Defensive alignments, which are usually selected by the defensive coordinator of the coaching staff, are made in response to the offensive formation on each play or what the defense thinks the offense's play will be. Sometimes the defensive coordinator/staff refers to a **frequency chart** to try to figure out what the offense will do. The frequency chart has a record of what types of plays the offense generally uses in particular situations (i.e., the number of times the team runs on first down, the number of times it passes on third down and short yardage, etc.).

Some football strategists believe that although offensive, defensive, and special team players must all possess good athletic skills, defensive players need to have more physical and tactical abilities than the members of the other two squads. Do you know why?

OFFENSE VS. DEFENSE

Keep in mind that when a player plays defense, he must respond immediately to an unknown situation. His offensive counterpart, on the other hand, finds himself in a relatively stable situation, one in which he knows and executes a precisely defined assignment.

The offensive player appears to have distinct advantages over his opponent on every play:
- He knows exactly what his assignment is.
- He knows precisely where he is to line up.
- He knows precisely when the ball will be snapped to begin the play.

Taking these factors into consideration, where does that leave the defensive player?

As you might have guessed, since the defense doesn't know exactly what formation it will use until the moment it lines up opposite the offense, it must react immediately and adjust accordingly, rather than going through the predetermined steps of a specific play like the offense can. Since the defense doesn't know exactly when the play is going to start, it is momentarily at a disadvantage when the ball is finally snapped. Also, keep in mind that the offense uses certain plays and maneuvers that are specifically designed to mislead the defense. When these fakes are used, a defensive player may be out of position; as a result, the offense may have another advantage.

As you can see, then, the flexibility of the defense is extremely important. Since the defense is somewhat disadvantaged at the start of every play because it doesn't know the exact game plan, it must be extremely aggressive in order to overcome that disadvantage with good physical skills, mental agility, flexibility, and determination.

DEFENSIVE ALIGNMENTS

There is a wide variety of defensive alignments used in football. Within each of these defensive patterns, however, are three common components: 1) **defensive linemen**, also called **down** or **interior linemen**; 2) **linebackers**; and 3) **defensive backs**. In the defense, alignments are commonly designated by the number of linemen, linebackers, and defensive backs, in that order.

What does that mean? The alignments are actually almost self-explanatory. Very simply, the digits in a defensive alignment refer to the number of players in a particular position:

- The first digit refers to the number of defensive linemen.
- The second digit refers to the number of linebackers.
- The third digit refers to the number of defensive backs.

Most defensive alignments are described by only two digits, although some contain three or more to include the defensive backs. When you hear announcers refer to a specific alignment, they will generally only use two digits.

Given the above information, can you guess, then, for example, what a **4-3-4** defense is? Yes, it's an alignment which has four defensive linemen, three linebackers, and four defensive backs.

Now that you understand what the numbers mean, let's take a look at the most common basic alignments. We'll start with the **4-3-4** defense, usually referred to as the **4-3** defense.

4-3 Defense

In a **4-3** defense, the basic defense in professional football, you will see four defensive linemen, three linebackers, and four defensive backs. The advantage of the 4-3 is that it's a balanced defense that can meet most of the challenges of the offense and can put considerable pressure on the quarterback. This type of defense can defend well against both passing and running plays.

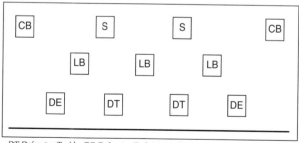

DT-Defensive Tackle, DE-Defensive End, LB-Linebacker, S-Safety, CB-Cornerback

7.1 4-3 Defense

3-4 Defense

The **3-4** defense, which has three defensive linemen, four linebackers, and four defensive backs, is used when the defense expects a passing play from the offense. The four linebackers and four defensive backs provide extra pass defense/coverage for receivers. In the 3-4 defense, three linemen rush the quarterback and the fourth linebacker keeps the offense guessing as to what he will do. The offense doesn't know what to expect: will the linebacker rush the quarterback, or will he drop back to provide pass coverage? This uncertainty for the offense at times provides an advantage for the defense.

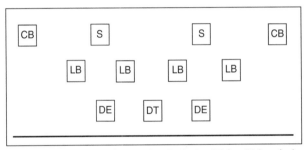

DT-Defensive Tackle, DE-Defensive End, LB-Linebacker, S-Safety, CB-Cornerback

7.2 3-4 DEFENSE

Nickel Defense

In situations where the offense is likely to pass, the defense sometimes uses a **nickel defense** (also called the **nickel package**) which involves five defensive backs instead of the usual four to provide extra pass coverage. The fifth defensive back in this alignment is called the **nickel back**.

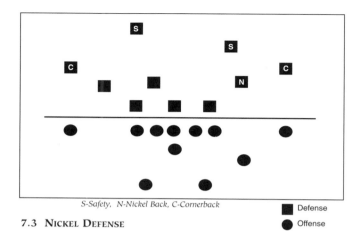

S-Safety, N-Nickel Back, C-Cornerback

Defense

Offense

7.3 NICKEL DEFENSE

Dime Defense

The **dime defense** (also called the **dime package**) uses six defensive backs for pass coverage, is another alignment used when the defense expects a passing play. The sixth defensive back, as you probably have already guessed, is called the **dime back**.

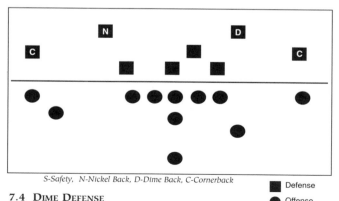

S-Safety, N-Nickel Back, D-Dime Back, C-Cornerback

Defense

Offense

7.4 DIME DEFENSE

Goal Line Defense

When the offense is inside the defense's 5 yard line and is about to score a touchdown, the defense sometimes uses a goal line defense. Since the defense believes that the offense will try to score with a running play, it brings in six or more players to prevent the ball carrier from gaining too much yardage or scoring.

Prevent Defense

This defense involves trying to prevent the offense from completing passes and advancing the ball to win the game in the last two minutes of the first half of the game. The defense positions only three linemen to rush the quarterback and has eight players back for pass coverage. The rationale behind the prevent defense is to allow short passes to be completed and to tackle the receivers before they can get out of bounds and stop the clock. This prevent defense allows short gains to be made, but it guards against long completions. You will generally see the prevent defense used late in the game when the defense is winning the game and the offense is trying to catch up.

DEFENSIVE PLAYS

As I previously explained, defenses begin every play at somewhat of a disadvantage. In trying to overcome this disadvantage, defenses at times attack first rather than react to something that the offense puts before them. Some of the most common strategies a defense uses to force the action on the field are described below:

Blitz

The **blitz**, referred to by some as one of the game's most spectacular sights, occurs when linebackers and defensive backs, or the defensive backs individually, charge the offensive line to tackle or sack the quarterback behind the line of scrimmage.

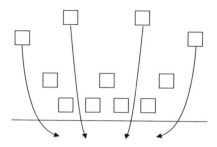

7.5 BLITZ

Here are a couple of other terms directly related to blitzing:

Safety Blitz

A safety blitz is a sudden charge made by one of the safeties in an attempt to tackle the quarterback.

Blitz Out of the Nickel

This is a pass rush when there is a nickel defensive alignment (five defensive backs).

Blitz Out of the Dime

This is a pass rush when there is a dime defensive alignment (six defensive backs).

Showing Blitz

A showing blitz is used to describe the defensive alignment before the ball is snapped. It means that the defensive formation (either the linebackers or the defensive backs) indicates it may blitz once the play begins.

Reading the Blitz

This is the offense's reaction to the defensive alignment. If the quarterback "reads the blitz," he suspects that the linebackers and/or defensive backs are going to rush in to sack him. If he reads the blitz early enough before the ball is snapped, he can audibilize (change the play at the line of scrimmage) to make adjustments and hopefully avoid being sacked.

Slant and **stack** are two other terms you'll hear which are directly related to the defense.

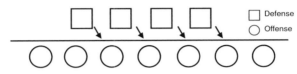

7.6 SLANT

Slant

When the ball is snapped, the defensive linemen charge at an angle or **slant** to the right or the left instead of straight ahead. Using this strategy gives the linebackers and the defensive backs a good opportunity to attack the offense.

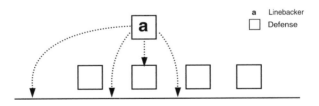

7.7 STACK

Stack

Stacking refers to one or more of the linebackers lining up directly behind the defensive linemen. **Stacking** the linebackers is like hiding them to keep them away from the offensive linemen. As you might expect, the stack poses a problem to the offensive linemen who do not know where the linebacker is going to charge; they are not sure whether the linebacker will go to the left, to the right, or charge straight ahead.

PASS DEFENSE

In order for a team to have a solid overall defense, it must have a defensive secondary (pass defenders) to provide excellent pass coverage. Pass coverage is a difficult assignment for defenders; it means that they must run with the receivers and prevent them from catching passes. Defenses use two major types of pass coverages: **man-to-man**, sometimes called **man-for-man**, and **zone**.

Man-to-Man Defense

This is the simplest of the pass defenses. In a **man-to-man** defense, defensive backs and linebackers play against (**cover**) a specific running back or receiver to whom they have been assigned. Each pass defender meets his specific receiver as the receiver leaves the line

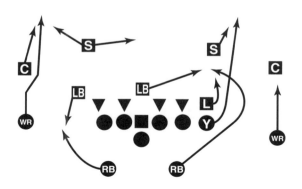

C-Cornerback, S-Safety, LB-Linebacker, WR-Wide Receiver, RB-Running Back, Y-Tight End

7.8 MAN-TO-MAN DEFENSE

of scrimmage and then stays with him until the play is over.

How do pass defenders know who to cover in a man-to-man alignment? Usually the assignments are given to the defensive backs and linebackers in the following way:

- The strong safety defends against the tight end.
- The free safety plays the wandering role; he is available to help his other teammates.
- The cornerbacks defend against the wide receivers.
- The linebackers cover the running backs.

Playing man-to-man defense can be difficult for the pass defender; he must keep his eyes on the jersey number of his specific receiver until the receiver makes his final move. When the pass is in the air traveling toward the receiver, the pass defender must carefully position himself to be able to step in front of the receiver to deflect or take the ball away (intercept or **pick off**) without interfering with the receiver. If he can't get to the ball, then he must be able to tackle the receiver who makes the catch.

When playing man-to-man coverage, the pass defender wants to make sure that he is never **burned**, that is, never makes an error in his pass coverage to allow "his" receiver to catch a long pass, make a long run, or score a touchdown (the worst case scenario).

Zone Defense

In order for a defense to be successful, it must have quickness, strength, solid tackling, good man-to-man coverage, and sound coverage of various parts of the field known as **zones.** The zones are not actually marked on the football field, but experienced pass defenders know the limits of their own zone or territory.

The **zone defense** is a defense using an imaginary group of zones on the field. Instead of being assigned to

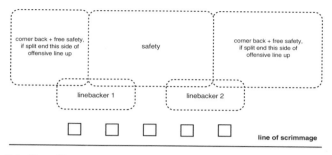

| corner back + free safety, if split end this side of offensive line up | safety | corner back + free safety, if split end this side of offensive line up |

| linebacker 1 | linebacker 2 |

□ □ □ □ □ **line of scrimmage**

7.9 ZONE DEFENSE

cover a particular receiver, as in man-to-man coverage, zone defense calls for each pass defender to follow a receiver that moves into a particular zone. The basic theory behind the zone defense is to get every area or zone covered adequately; this type of defense works best in preventing the offense from completing long bombs. When a team uses a zone defense, the announcers frequently use the term "**seam.**" The seam refers to the area on the football field where two zones meet.

It is important to remember that whether a player is playing "man-to-man" or "zone," he must be careful about the **pass interference** penalty. He must make sure that in pursuing the ball, he doesn't contact the receiver too soon; that is, he can't touch the receiver before the ball arrives or he will be guilty of pass interference.

7.10 PASS INTERFERENCE

HOW TO WATCH THE DEFENSE

Now that we have gone through the basics of defensive play, it's time to apply what you've learned to an actual game situation. If you are watching a game on television, you may be operating at a disadvantage. Why? Television cameras rarely show much of the defensive team. However, as teams break out of their huddles, observe how they line up. If you're unsure of player positions, turn back to Chapter 2 and refer to the jersey numbering system to help you. Then try to answer the following questions:

- How many defensive linemen (jersey numbers 60-79, 90-99) are on the line of scrimmage? This gives you a clue as to what the defense is expecting from the offense. If the defense expects a running play, there will be more linemen. If it expects a passing play, there will be fewer linemen.

- How many linebackers (jersey numbers 50-59, 90-99) are there, and where are they positioned? Are they directly behind the linemen, or alongside them to stop a possible running play? Or are they positioned back to serve as pass defenders? Are there any linebackers positioned on or lurking near the line of scrimmage for a possible blitz on the quarterback?

- How are the defensive backs (jersey numbers 20-49) lined up? Is one near his defensive linemen on the line of scrimmage? If he is, that might indicate he is going to charge in on a safety blitz to tackle the quarterback.

As mentioned in the previous chapter, when the ball is snapped, try not to watch only the progress of the ball. If you look at the offensive formations, defensive alignments, and movement of players away from the ball, you will understand and enjoy the game more.

✓ CHAPTER 7 CHECKLIST
THINGS TO REMEMBER

- Defenses: 4-3, 3-4, nickel, dime, goal line, prevent
- Defensive plays: blitz, stack, slant
- Pass defense: man-to-man, zone

TERMS TO KNOW

| alignment | dime back | pick off |
| burned | nickel back | seam |

EXTRA POINTS: DID YOU KNOW?

- The most one-sided football game ever played was the National Football League championship game in 1940 in which the Chicago Bears defeated the Washington Redskins by a score of 73-0. The Bears gained 372 yards while the Redskins' total output was 3! The Bears scored 11 touchdowns by 10 different players, and 6 different players made 7 conversions.

- Defensive great Jim Marshall of the Minnesota Vikings made national headlines in 1961 in a game against the San Francisco 49ers. During the game, he scooped up a fumble and raced 60 yards in the wrong direction! Marshall crossed the goal line thinking he had scored a touchdown for his Vikings, but in fact he scored a safety for the 49ers. The Vikings, however, still won the game with a score of 27-22.

CHAPTER 8

SPECIAL TEAMS

"What do these guys do that's so special?" - Joan Fenn (1993)

Special teams, units that perform specific functions, make up the third team in football, in addition to the offense and defense. Although generally underrated and sometimes overlooked by the fans, special teams contribute a great deal to a football team.

The term "special teams," sometimes known as **"suicide squads,"** does not refer to a single unit; in fact, every football team has several special teams, those teams which come into the game for kicking situations: **kickoff team, kick return team, punting team, punt return team, field goal unit** and **extra point unit.**

When special teams enter the game, one of the following three things happen:
• The play will involve a change in possession of the football.
• The play will involve a large amount of yardage, usually 40 yards or more.
• The play will be an attempt to score points.

Let's take a look at each of these special teams and their responsibilities.

KICKOFF TEAM

When kicking off, the kicking team has one thing on its mind: to kick the ball deep into the receiving team's territory and to contain the ball carrier deep in that territory. A good kicker will keep the ball in the air as long as possible to give his teammates sufficient time to move downfield to tackle the **kick returner,** who is usually positioned about 60 yards away from the kicker. In addition to giving the ball height, a good kicker will also try to get the ball to bounce and roll, making it difficult for the kick returner to catch and advance. The kicker must have a good defensive team which will move downfield quickly and respond well to changes in the direction of the receiving team's movement, especially that of the player who catches the ball.

On the kickoff, every member of the kicking team is assigned a lane of coverage. When the kicker kicks the ball (which is held upright by a kicking tee), his teammates race downfield, keeping aware of their particular lanes. Special teams' coaches like to see members of their kickoff teams **gang-tackle** the kick returner because this type of tackling (involving several players bringing down one opponent) increases the chances of a fumble occurring, and the kicking team's recovering the football close to the receiving team's goal line.

The kickoff team will be on the field several times during a game: at the start of the game; at the start of the second half; after each point after touchdown attempt; after a field goal has been scored; and after a safety has been scored.

All kickoffs take place on the kicking team's 30-yard line (except after a 2-point safety has been scored) or unless a foul has been committed and a penalty is assessed on the kickoff. At kickoff, all members of the kicking team must be behind the 30-yard line, while all members of the receiving team must be at least 10 yards away from the ball. A kickoff going out of bounds between the goal lines is placed on the receiving team's 40-yard line. The receiving team then begins its series of plays from that spot, or from the spot where the ball went out of bounds.

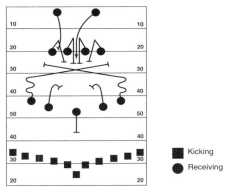

8.1 KICKOFF

■ Kicking
● Receiving

Onside Kick

Occasionally a team (which is losing late in a game and has just scored) tries to keep possession of the football by using an **onside kick**. An onside kick is a short kickoff maneuver used by the kicking team in hopes that the receiving team will mishandle the awkward rolling or bouncing ball. If the ball travels at least 10 yards, either team can take immediate possession. If the kicking team is able to recover either the untouched or the mishandled ball after an onside kick, it is in a better field position for scoring than it would have been had the kick traveled to the far end of the field. As with a kickoff, all onside kicks take place on the kicking team's 30-yard line.

Since the kicking team plans where the ball is to land, it has about a 50-50 chance of recovering it. The team expecting the onside kick puts in players who have the best ball-handling skills (sometimes called the **hands**

team), the receivers and running backs. Just remember the rule of the onside kick: as long as the ball travels at least 10 yards, either team, not just the receiving team, can take possession.

Safety Free Kick

In addition to a kickoff, another free kick is used during a game: a kick after a safety. On a free kick after a safety, the team scored upon (the offense) must give the ball over to the defense. The offense must kick the ball from its own 20-yard line, but has the option of punting it or placekicking it without the use of a tee.

KICK RETURN TEAM (RECEIVING TEAM)

The main goal of the **kick return team**, the team that receives the kick, is to set up their offensive team to begin play on at least their own 20-yard line.

A kick return team is separated into three groups: five blockers, a four-man wedge, and two kick returners, sometimes called **deep men.** At the time of the kickoff, the four-man wedge falls back and becomes a block for the kick returner to run behind. The kick return team has to keep an eye out for the **"wedgebuster,"** the player on the kicking team who arrives downfield first to break up the wedge and get to the kick returner. The kick returner follows the wedge of blockers until he sees an opening, then he runs upfield without the benefit of blocking teammates. During a kick return, the returner will try to find a hole in the kickoff team's defense and try to advance the ball as far as he possibly can. One of the most exciting plays in football is a long kickoff return, or one in which the kick returner scores a touchdown. It doesn't happen often, but when it does, it's a sight to see.

Usually the last defender that the kick returner meets on his way upfield is the kicker. When the kick returner gets to that point, he has a good chance of returning the kick **"all the way"** for a touchdown (sometimes this is referred to as **"taking it to the house"**) since kickers are not generally known for their tackling abilities. If a kickoff team allows a kick returner to penetrate its defense to a point where he meets the kicker on his way upfield, the special team has suffered a great humiliation. And, to add insult to injury, if the kicker doesn't tackle the kick returner, the kick return team usually scores 6 points.

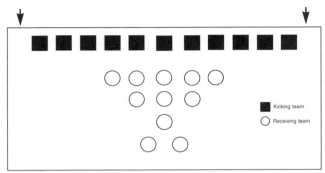

8.2 Kick Return Team

PUNTING TEAM

The **punting team** performs duties similar to those of the kickoff team. The main difference is the position of the football when it is kicked. On a kickoff, the ball is kicked from a kicking tee placed on the ground. A punt is kicked after the ball is dropped from the punter's hands.

Why and when is a punt used? When the offense is faced with a fourth down situation, is out of field goal range, and cannot gain the yardage necessary for a first down, it must use the kicking maneuver known as a punt. By using a punt, the offense gives the defense the ball deep in the defense's territory, often very close to the defense's goal line.

To execute a punt, the punter lines up about 15 yards behind the line of scrimmage. The linemen in front of him protect the punter from being tackled. The special center used in punting situations is called the **long snapper**, and he snaps the ball back to the punter. The punter

makes sure that the laces on the football are facing up, drops the ball, then kicks it off the top of his foot as quickly as possible before the ball hits the ground. He has to be sure he doesn't **shank it**, meaning to kick the ball off the side of his foot, thus causing the punted ball to travel erratically for only a short distance. As you can imagine, shanking the ball is a punter's nightmare.

8.3 PUNTER

In order for a smooth punt, the punter must quickly kick the ball. Under ideal conditions, the snap should take eight-tenths of a second; the punter's kick should take another 1.3 seconds. If the combined snap and kick takes any longer than 2.1 seconds, then the punter risks oncoming members of the punt return team blocking his punt. Some special teams' coaches prefer having their punters kick shorter but very high kicks so that the punt returner is completely surrounded by members of the punting team as soon as he catches the ball.

Like the placekicker, a punter likes to have about four seconds of hang time in order to give his teammates sufficient time to move downfield and tackle the punt returner as quickly as possible after he has caught the ball. But unlike the kicker who is never rushed and whose opponents are always 10 yards away from him, the punter has to contend with charging opponents all intent on blocking his punt.

8.3 PUNTER

The punter usually tries to kick the ball very near his opponent's goal line, but not into the end zone. Why?

Any time the ball goes untouched into the end zone on a kickoff or punt, it is a **touchback**. After a touchback, the ball is automatically placed on the 20-yard line for the next play. Instead of having the ball land in the end zone, it would be better for the punting team to have the ball go out of bounds within the 20-yard line or the punt returner downed between the goal line and the 20-yard line. With either of these scenarios, the receiving team would be deeper in its own territory with poorer field position. Members of the punting team often race downfield trying to catch an untouched ball and **down it** as close as possible to the receiving team's goal line. When that happens, the receiving team must take possession of the ball at that spot.

A way for punting teams to contain their opponents deep in their own territory is by having their punter kick a **straight away punt**, a punt that is kicked as high and as far as possible. However, a punter may decide against kicking straight away, and instead decide to kick a **pooch punt** or a **coffin corner punt**. When the punter kicks a pooch punt, it is very high and comes down within the receiving team's 5-yard line. The objective of a coffin corner punt is for the ball to land in one of the corners where the sideline meets the goal line (coffin corner) and bounce out of bounds. If done successfully, these three types of punts are excellent strategies which force the receiving team to begin play deep in its own territory.

PUNT RETURN TEAM

Unlike the kick return team, a **punt return team** has the major responsibility to try to prevent the punter from making a successful punt. Their game plan is for several players to rush against one part of the blocking offensive line in an attempt to get to the punter.

Roughing the Kicker

When members of the punt return team are able to break through the offensive line and have a chance of tackling the punter, they must be aware of the **roughing the kicker** rule. If any player flagrantly runs into the punter without touching the ball in the process, the punt return team is penalized. The penalty for roughing the kicker is 15 yards plus an automatic first down. This foul results in the kicking team's keeping the ball because of the automatic first down rule; since the kicking team now has a first down, it no longer has to punt the ball to its opponent. If someone **runs into** the kicker, the penalty is 5 yards. Therefore, it is obvious how important it is that the rushing blockers do not rough the kicker.

However, it is a different story if the punter gets tackled or blocked, and his punt is touched or blocked. If the ball is touched or hits the ground, there is no penalty for roughing the kicker.

Sometimes a charging player slightly touches the punter, and the punter gives an Academy Award-winning performance. He might fall on the ground, hoping that the referee will throw a penalty marker for roughing the kicker resulting in the punting team keeping the ball instead of punting it to its opponents. Sometimes these performances backfire and the punter gets himself into trouble; not only doesn't he get the desired response of the referee throwing a penalty marker for roughing the kicker, but the punter himself gets penalized. The NFL rules state that a punter, placekicker, or holder who simulates being roughed or run into by a defensive player can be penalized 15 yards.

Like members of the kickoff team, the punt return team provides protection for its punt return man. Since it is difficult for the punt returner to run up the middle of the field with his opponents in position when he catches the ball, he usually runs behind a wall of his blockers to the right or the left side of the field.

Fair Catch

With the punt airborne traveling toward him, the punt returner has a decision to make. In the few seconds he has, he watches the opposing punting team running full speed to surround him, and asks himself the following questions:

- Do I let this ball go untouched into our end zone, resulting in it being brought out only to our own 20-yard line?

- Do I attempt to catch this punt and take a chance of getting tackled immediately?

- Is there some room to advance the ball?

- Do I signal for a fair catch?

He has a lot of thinking to do in just a few seconds of hang time!

If he allows the ball to go into the end zone, he is, in a sense, denying himself and his teammates the opportunity of having better field position farther upfield than the 20-yard line. If he lets the ball go over his head, and it doesn't go all the way into the end zone but goes out of bounds, his teammates have to take over the ball in a poor field position at a spot back deeper than their own 20-yard line. Also, if the ball goes over his head, he may run the risk of having his opponents catch it and down it very close to his own goal line.

If he decides to catch the punt knowing that his opponents have already arrived downfield and are ready to pounce on him as soon as he catches it, he may run the risk of fumbling the ball. If he touches the ball in any way without taking possession or fumbles it deep in his own territory, his opponents may recover and be in good scoring position.

His last option involves giving the signal for a **fair catch**. While a punt is still in flight, the return man must clearly indicate he is making a fair catch by raising one arm straight above his head and waving it from side to side. A fair catch means that when he catches the ball, he will not be interfered with by the members of the punting team. Even if he signals a fair catch, he is not required to catch the ball. A fair catch can also be used during a kickoff, although it is rarely used.

Incorrect
Fair Catch Signal

Correct
Fair Catch Signal

8.4 FAIR CATCH

However, once the punt returner makes a signal for a fair catch, he is not allowed to advance the ball farther than two steps upfield. He must give a clear fair catch signal or he can be penalized 5 yards. If he has given a clear fair catch signal and one of his opponents tackles him, bumps him, or runs into him, the kicking team is penalized for **fair catch interference**. Once the fair catch is made in either a punting or a kickoff situation, the receiving team starts from the point where the catch is made.

Whenever a punting situation is about to take place, pay special attention to the punter and the punt return man. While learning the game, you'll get to understand most of the punt action by focusing your attention on these two key players.

FIELD GOAL UNIT

The **field goal unit** will come onto the field when the offense has a fourth down and does not want to take the risk of failing to gain the yardage necessary for a new first down. Before a team decides to attempt a field goal instead of punting to its opponents, the coaching staff considers several things:

The team's field position:

- Are we in our own territory or in our opponents'?
- If we miss this field goal, will we be giving our opponents an easy opportunity to score?
- Are our opponents' goal posts within range of our kicker?

Weather conditions:

- Will the direction and strength of the wind help or hinder us when we try to kick this field goal? Are we kicking into the wind or with the wind?
- Can our holder handle a slippery or frozen football?

The kicker:

- Is he free from injuries and operating at full capacity?
- What is his current field goal percentage from this range?
- Has he ever kicked a field goal further than what he would be attempting?

The kicker and his holder work together to assure that the ball is kicked in at least 1.3 seconds. Taking more time would risk having the field goal blocked. After receiving the centered ball approximately 7 yards behind the line of scrimmage, the holder, while down on one knee, positions the ball on the ground for the kicker to kick over the crossbar of the opponent's goal post. If the ball goes over the crossbar, or if it touches the crossbar or one of the uprights and then drops behind the crossbar, it is "good" and the field goal unit scores 3 points. If, on the other hand, the ball travels wide to the right or to the left of an upright, hits an upright or the crossbar, but does not drop behind the crossbar, then the field goal is "no good."

Missed Field Goals

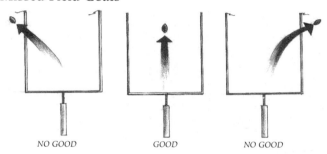

NO GOOD   GOOD   NO GOOD

8.5 Field Goals

What happens if the kicking team misses a field goal? An NFL rule enacted in 1994 states that if a team attempts and misses a field goal beyond the defense's 20-yard line, the defensive team takes over possession of the ball at the spot where the holder held the ball for the attempt (the spot of the miss), not at the line of scrimmage (the spot of the snap) as was done in the past. If a field goal is attempted and missed from within the defense's 20-yard line, the ball will revert to the defensive team at the 20-yard line. The new rule gives the ball back to the defense 7 yards closer to the offensive team's goal line. It will undoubtedly discourage offenses from attempting very long field goals, when the chances of missing are greater.

The defense, in trying to prevent a field goal, has responsibilities similar to the punt return team in that it must try to block the kick or try to prevent the kicker from making the kick without getting a penalty for roughing the kicker in the process. Lastly, it must try to safeguard against the holder, usually a quarterback, from running a **fake field goal**. This is a play originally set up to be a field goal attempt, but turns out to be a running or a passing play. Instead of putting the ball on the ground for the kicker to kick, the holder may hand the ball off to a running back, throw the ball, or run with the ball himself in an attempt to gain the first down yardage.

Seeing a fake field goal is one of the more exciting plays in football. The team attempting the fake field goal risks losing a sure 3 points, especially if the field goal attempt was a short one, for a chance to earn enough yardage for a first down, keep the ball, then have a chance to score a touchdown for 6 points. Since fake field goals are not attempted too often, they are fun plays to watch, especially when they're successful.

Sometimes fake field goal plays are not intentionally fakes. For example, the field goal unit may have every intention of actually kicking a field goal. However, if there is a **"bad snap"** from the center to the holder (i.e., the ball goes over his head or hits the ground) and the ball can't be positioned properly and quickly for the kicker, the holder may opt for a fake field goal play. Sometimes these unplanned fake field goals have surprising results for the offense, the defense, or both.

EXTRA POINT UNIT

You will see the **extra point unit** come on to the field immediately after their team (either the offense or defense) has scored a touchdown. This special unit has responsibilities similar to the field goal unit; the placekicker and holder must work together so that the ball is kicked quickly. When attempting an extra point, the ball is placed on the 2-yard line of the defense, then snapped back to the holder who holds it upright on the ground for the kicker at the 10-yard line.

Remember that the goal posts are 10 yards away from the goal line. Therefore, an extra point attempt is actually the same as a 20-yard field goal. Although most will agree that extra point attempts are almost always successful (the average NFL team makes 95% of its extra point/PAT attempts), sometimes they are blocked, miskicked, or the holder mishandles the ball. Missed extra points play a crucial role in a game; teams have lost games due to missed extra points. Announcers often refer to missed extra points as "one of those things that can come back to haunt you." Even something as seemingly easy to execute as an extra point can never be taken for granted.

2-POINT CONVERSION UNIT

This unit may line up like a regular offensive unit trying to score a touchdown by pass or run from the defensive team's 2-yard line, but instead of scoring a touchdown worth 6 points, the team will either pass or carry the ball into the end zone for a 2-point score.

According to Joe Avezzano, the special teams coach of the Dallas Cowboys, "The kicking game is now used as a weapon to the point where you can win a couple of games a year just because of it. Most teams have somebody who can **take it to the house** on you on any given play." His counterpart for the Washington Redskins, Pete Rodriguez, says that "there is no other play in football that can turn the ball game one way or another." Although members of the offense and defense may be highlighted in the media more often, it is easy to recognize the enormous contribution special teams make to the overall success of a football team.

CHAPTER 8 CHECKLIST
THINGS TO REMEMBER

SPECIAL TEAMS

extra point unit
field goal unit
kickoff return team

kickoff team
punt return team
punting

TERMS TO KNOW

coffin corner punt
fair catch

fake field goal
hang time
straight away punt

onside kick
pooch punt

EXTRA POINTS: DID YOU KNOW?

- According to the **Official National Football League 1992 Record and Fact Book**, the record for kicking the longest punt is held by Steve O'Neal of the New York Jets. On September 21, 1969, in a game against the Denver Broncos, O'Neal, who also played as a wide receiver, kicked a punt that traveled 98 yards.

- On October 23, 1994, Robert Bailey of the Los Angeles Rams broke an NFL record by returning a punt 103 yards for a touchdown against the New Orleans Saints.

- If you ever think your daily schedule is hectic or challenging, consider the schedule of Deion "Prime Time" Sanders, who plays both professional football and major league baseball. One day in 1993, Sanders tried to play both sports. He played center fielder for his former team, the Atlanta Braves, against the Philadelphia Phillies in a National League baseball playoff game. Afterwards, Sanders flew to Atlanta, where that evening he and his former teammates, the Atlanta Falcons, beat the Los Angeles Rams 30-24.

CHAPTER 9

OFFICIALS

"The striped team on the field always wins, doesn't it?"
- Lynda P. (1985)

Professional football games are supervised by a staff of "zebra-striped" **officials** provided by the National Football League who oversee play and enforce the rules. Each of the seven officials is positioned at a different spot on the field and has particular duties. Although the **referee,** the chief official, has general charge of the game and the final word on all rulings, any of the officials may call a rule violation. This chapter sketches the responsibilities of each member of the officiating crew.

Official's Uniform

From head to toe, each official's uniform consists of black and white, starting a black baseball-type cap with white stripes, except for the referee, who wears a white cap; black and white striped shirt, black belt, white knicker pants, black and white striped socks, and black shoes. There are white letters and numbers on the front and back of each official's shirt that help the spectators to identify them. The letters reflect his job (i.e., R=referee, U=umpire, etc.), while the numbers correspond with his name in the game program roster. Unlike the players, NFL officials have no required numbering system, so an official may have a different number each year. All officials carry a whistle, a weighted bright gold flag, and an NFL Officials' Game Card on which he records every foul and penalty he signals during a game.

In the diagram below, notice that each official positions himself at a different place on the field for the beginning of each play. Each official covers a specific area of the field and looks for particular types of infractions. The following is a list of each official's duties and his location on the field.

Some of the words in **bold** type may be unfamiliar to you. Don't worry; they are penalties and will be discussed at greater length in Chapter 10.

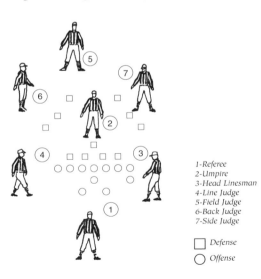

1-*Referee*
2-*Umpire*
3-*Head Linesman*
4-*Line Judge*
5-*Field Judge*
6-*Back Judge*
7-*Side Judge*

☐ *Defense*
◯ *Offense*

9.1 OFFICIALS

Referee (RF-1)

The referee is the chief official who wears a wireless microphone and takes a position in the backfield 10 to 12 yards behind the line of scrimmage. He tends to favor the right side if the quarterback is right handed. He is responsible for making all calls, even though some other official may have spotted a rule violation.

Responsibilities include:

- Announcing all rule violations
- Notifying coaches of the **two minute warning** and when they have used all their time outs
- Ruling on **fumbles**
- Watching the quarterback and ruling on **roughing the quarterback**
- Keeping track of and signaling the number of downs
- Overseeing the **coin toss**
- Announcing options on penalties, unless they are automatic
- Signaling when to start and stop the game clock

Umpire (U-2)

The umpire takes up his position four to five yards behind the defensive line, varying his position from in front of weakside tackle to strongside guard, and makes sure no infringements take place in that area.

Responsibilities include:

- Watching for **false starts** of offensive linemen
- Watching for contact between players on the line of scrimmage
- Ruling whether passes were completed or **trapped**
- Watching for **ineligible pass receivers** downfield
- Checking equipment of players

Head Linesman (HL-3)

The head linesman positions himself on the line of scrimmage.

Responsibilities include:

- Looking for **offside**, **encroachment**, and actions pertaining to the scrimmage line on his side of the line before or at the snap
- Assisting referee in keeping track of downs
- Watching the closest running back, blockers, and defenders on his side of the field
- Ensuring that the **chain crew/gang** carries out its duties correctly
- Watching for illegal receivers

Line Judge (LJ-4)

The line judge positions himself on the line of scrimmage opposite the head linesman.

Responsibilities include:

- Watching for **offside**, **encroachment** and actions pertaining to the scrimmage line on his side of the field
- Watching the kicking team charge down the field during a kickoff or punt
- Timing the game as back up to the official clock operator/time keeper
- Watching the plays (blockers and defenders) on his side of the field
- Watching the quarterback to make sure the pass is thrown from behind, not beyond, the line of scrimmage
- Firing a starter pistol to signal the end of each period
- Counting members of the offensive team

Field Judge (FJ-5)

The field judge positions himself 25 yards deep in the defense.

Responsibilities include:

- Checking validity of passes, punt catches, and fair catches
- Making decisions on field goals and extra points
- Watching for **pass interference** violations
- Keeping his eye on the tight end
- Watching for illegal substitutions
- Checking the kicker and height of the kicking tee
- Counting members of the defensive team on the field at the snap

Back Judge (BJ-6)

The back judge is positioned 20 yards back from the line of scrimmage near the sideline on the same side of the field as the line judge.

Responsibilities include:

- Helping the field judge decide on extra points, kicks, and field goals
- Spotting violations between defensive backs and pass receivers (i.e., pass interference)
- Making decisions on out of bounds/in bounds on sideline plays near his side of the field
- Spotting **clipping** violations on punt returns
- Making decisions involving catching, recovery, or illegal touching of a loose ball beyond the line of scrimmage
- Counting the number of defensive players on the field at the snap

Side Judge (SJ-7)

The side judge stands 20 yards from the line of scrimmage opposite the back judge and on the same side of the field as the head linesman.

Responsibilities include:

- Making decisions involving the sideline on his side of the field
- Ruling on plays involving pass receivers
- Ruling on **pass interference**
- Watching the wide receiver on his side of the field

Chain Crew/Gang

The seven-member chain crew assists the seven officials with the operations of the game, provided by the home team and approved by the NFL. It is usually made up of two **rodmen,** one **boxman,** one **clipman,** one person to handle the forward stake indicator, one **drive start marker,** and one substitute chain crew member.

9.2 Chain Crew/Gang

Rodmen

The two chain crew members called rodmen manage a metal chain 10 yards in length with a metal rod attached to each end of the chain: one rodman holds the rod at the line where the offense began its previous first down play. The second rodman, 10 yards away, holds the pole which marks the spot to which the team must advance for a new first down. The rodmen do not move until the 10 yards are gained. When measuring for a first down, if the tip of the ball touches the pole or extends beyond it, it is a first down; the referee indicates this by pointing in the direction of the defense's goal line.

Boxman

The boxman handles the **down marker/indicator**, a four-foot pole with four signs numbered 1, 2, 3, and 4 for the four downs. The down marker marks the most forward point of the ball at the start of every play and displays the number of the down. The boxman flips over the appropriate sign at the start of every play.

Clipman

The clipman places a "clip" with a dial on it at the midpoint of the 10-yard chain. For example, if a team has a first down on the 38-yard line, it must get to the 48-yard line for a new first down. When the chains are set at this location on the field, the clipman places a clip at the midpoint of the chain and sets the dial to read 43. This clipping procedure is done so the officials always know exactly where the ball is on the field, even if the chains have to be moved in a hurry or even dropped at the sidelines to prevent oncoming players from tripping.

Forward Stake Indicator

A member of the chain crew is in charge of the forward stake indicator, a large, vinyl, brightly colored arrow. He places this arrow on the ground on the sideline to indicate the spot to which a team must reach for a first down. The forward stake indicator is of great help to both members of the offense and defense: it lets them clearly see the yardage needed for a first down.

Drive Start Marker

Another member of the chain crew handles the **drive start**, a long pole marked with a black circle and a large orange X. This marks the point where the offense first took possession of the ball. It is moved only when possession of the ball changes from one team to another. Suppose, for example, that a team first gets the ball on its own 20-yard line, as in the case of a touchback. Although the team may advance the ball up the field, the drive start stays at the 20-yard line so that the length of the team's **drive** (the distance it gains before scoring or turning the ball over to its opponent) can be accurately measured.

Although the performance of each of the officials is crucial in ensuring a well-supervised game, the one official to keep an eye on is the referee. The referee is the official seen most often, especially if you are watching a game on television. He is the one who announces all fouls, assesses penalties to the teams guilty of violations, and signals all rulings to the teams, coaching staff and spectators. Although there are literally dozens of signals you may see the referee use during a game, the ones included here are the most common.

Official's Signals

By watching the referee carefully and reviewing these explanations, before long you'll know what he is going to say before he actually says it. This is just a handful of all the signals used by the officials during a game; the majority of signals are used to indicate rule violations and to assess penalties. Many of these penalty signals will be discussed in Chapter 10.

Official's Signals

Touchdown,
field goal or a conversion
(placekick, run or pass)
has been made

Incomplete pass,
missed field goal or
extra point, play
over or penalty
refused

A safety has been scored

First down

Fourth down

Loss of down

Time out

Referee's time out

No time out/time is in

Pass juggled
inbounds and caught
out of bounds

Touchback

Uncatchable forward pass - Officials
determine that a pass was not able
to be caught by the intended receiver

124

☑ CHAPTER 9 CHECKLIST
THINGS TO REMEMBER

- Seven member officiating crew – supervises the game
- Referee – chief official

umpire	side judge
head linesman	back judge
line judge	field judge

- Chain crew/gang – assists the officials
- Official's signals you should recognize: score, first down, safety, an incomplete pass, a missed field goal, and time out.

TERMS TO KNOW

boxman	drive start	rodmen
clipman	10-yard chain	
down marker	forward stake indicator	

EXTRA POINTS: DID YOU KNOW?

According to Donna Poole Foehr in her book **Touchdown** (1993), officials with the National Football League have a one-year contract and can earn from $700 to $2400 per game depending upon League seniority. Those officials who receive the best ratings from the supervisor of officials are selected to officiate post-season games, where they receive $7,000 for each playoff game and $8,500 for the Super Bowl game.

CHAPTER 10

FLAG ON THE PLAY

"Daddy, why does everyone get so upset when that little yellow cloth is on the ground?" - Mary Beth Mooney (1968)

During a football game, some of the players break the rules and, as a result, get penalized for their actions. Since the responsibility of the officiating crew is to supervise the game, any time any official sees a foul, he must indicate it by throwing a weighted yellow handkerchief-sized cloth in the air. When this cloth, also called a **penalty marker** or **flag**, is on the ground, it means that there was a procedural violation or that a player in the area where the flag was thrown committed a foul. In most cases, a violation occurs during a play, and the officials allow the play to be completed.

When there is a **flag on the play**, several things will happen:

- The referee blows the whistle and the official clock is stopped.

- The official who threw the flag informs the referee which foul he spotted, as well as the jersey number of the player guilty of the violation.

- The officials discuss the penalty to be assessed and determine the options available to the team against which the foul was committed.

- The referee discusses the violation with the captain of the team against which the foul was committed and describes his options, unless the penalty is automatic.

- The referee uses signals to indicate which foul was committed and points to the team which committed the infraction. He then turns on his wireless microphone, announces the foul, the jersey number of the player guilty of the violation, whether the guilty player is a member of the offense or defense, whether the penalty was **declined** (refused), the yards penalized for the foul, and the number of the next down.

This series of events is what you will see and hear most often. Pay special attention to the body gestures and remarks of the referee at this time. He follows the same basic sequence each time there is a penalty.

Penalty Enforcement

A penalty is measured from four starting places, depending upon which foul was committed:

- Where the ball was last put into play (previous)

- Where the ball would be if the foul had not occurred (succeeding)

- The exact spot of the foul (exact)

- Where the foul-related action took place (spot of the snap, pass, fumble, return kick, or free kick)

When a team commits a foul, it may be penalized by a loss of yardage, a loss of down, and in some cases both, depending upon the seriousness of the foul. The team against which the foul was committed can also, in certain circumstances, be awarded an automatic first down. When both teams commit fouls on the same play, it results in **offsetting penalties.** That is, the penalties cancel each other out, and the down is repeated from the same spot on the field.

Just remember that penalties are not all treated in the same way and that they aren't all marked off from the same place. However, penalties all fall into the following categories:

- automatic first down
- loss of down (no yardage assessed)
- five yards and loss of a down
- five yards
- fifteen yards
- ten yards

- fifteen yards and automatic disqualification
- fifteen yards and an automatic first down
- fifteen yards and loss of coin toss option
- five yards and an automatic first down
- fifteen yards and disqualification/ejection (if flagrant)

Automatic First Down

Certain penalties, such as roughing the passer, roughing the kicker, and defensive pass interference, result in an automatic first down for the offensive team. It doesn't matter whether the foul is committed during a first, second, third, or fourth down play; these penalties still result in an automatic first down.

Suppose that the Indianapolis Colts, for example, have a fourth down and 6 yards to go from their own 50-yard line. Since it is out of the range for a field goal attempt, the Colts decide that they must punt to their opponents, the Detroit Lions. During the punt, one of the Lions' players charges into the punter (**roughs** him) without blocking the punted ball.

The Lions' player is guilty of **roughing the kicker.** The referee, seeing this infraction, throws the penalty marker to the ground. As a result of this penalty, Indianapolis gains 15 yards and, more importantly, receives an automatic first down. Now with a new first down, the Colts won't have to give the ball over to the Lions. So, in addition to getting to keep the ball with four more chances at making another first down, the Colts move 15 yards closer to the Detroit goal line.

Hopefully, it is now clearer why certain penalties have crucial consequences for the guilty team and why penalties have, on occasion, influenced the outcome of games.

Dead Ball Foul

Sometimes teams commit fouls before a play begins; these are called **dead ball fouls** because they occur when the ball is not in play, or dead. The following are a couple of common dead ball fouls:

Encroachment: This occurs when a player (with the exception of the center), usually a lineman, moves into the neutral zone and makes contact with an opposing player.

False Start: This occurs when an offensive player charges or moves in such a way as to simulate the start of a play after assuming a set position, but before the ball is snapped and the play actually begins.

If any part of a player's body extends beyond his line of scrimmage when the ball is snapped, then a common foul called an **offside** has been committed.

These fouls are rather common; in each instance the penalty for the infraction is 5 yards. The team that committed the foul loses this yardage and the down is replayed.

Accept vs. Refuse/Decline

When the referee indicates a foul has been committed against a particular team and the penalty does not result in an automatic first down, the captain of the team against which the foul was committed has two options:

- **Accept** the penalty to be imposed on the team guilty of the infraction.
- Refuse or **decline** (the term commonly used in football language) the penalty and accept the completed play.

If he accepts the penalty, the penalty yardage is enforced and the down is usually replayed. If the penalty is declined, or refused, then there is no yardage assessed and the down is not replayed just as if no penalty were involved.

Have I succeeded in thoroughly confusing you? I thought so. I realize this is a bit complicated, especially to newcomers to the game, so let's work through a couple of examples together.

Suppose the Atlanta Falcons have a first down and 10 yards to go from their own 30-yard line. The quarterback throws an incomplete pass that, of course, results in no gain. However, during this play, one of the Buffalo Bills' defensive linemen is guilty of encroachment, which results in a 5-yard penalty against Buffalo. What are Atlanta's options?

Since the Falcons did not gain any yardage on the play, the first down and 10 would normally (that is, without a penalty) become second down and 10 from the 30-yard line. However, there was a 5-yard penalty. If Atlanta's captains accept the penalty, 5 yards would be added to their field position (in a sense, taken away from Buffalo) and the ball would be put on the Atlanta 35-yard line instead of the 30.

OK so far? What happens, then, to the down? The rule is that if the penalty is accepted, the down is usually replayed. So, in our example, Atlanta would still have a first down, but with how many yards to go?

To calculate the yardage for the next play, subtract the penalty yardage (in Atlanta's case, 5 yards) from the previous number of yards to go (10 yards). 10 yards minus 5 yards of penalty = 5 yards to go. So instead of having 10 yards to go for another first down, Atlanta would have only 5 yards to go.

In another example, suppose the Chicago Bears have a second down and 9 yards to go from Cincinnati's 40-yard line. On a running play, the Bears gain 7 yards to the 33-yard line, and the Bengals are guilty of being offsides, which results in a 5-yard penalty. If the penalty is accepted, the ball is taken back to the original line of scrimmage (the 40-yard line) and moved 5 yards (the amount of the penalty) toward the guilty team's goal line. The ball would then be on Cincinnati's 35-yard line, which is 5 yards closer to the end zone.

Remember when a penalty is accepted, the same down is replayed, so it is still second down. Also remember to subtract the amount of the penalty from the previous yardage (9 yards minus 5 yards = 4 yards.) Originally, the Bears had 9 yards to go; because of the 5-yard penalty, now it is second down and 4 from the 35-yard line.

If Chicago chooses to decline the penalty, what would its situation be? When a team declines a penalty, the ball is left where it was when the play ended (in our case, the 33-yard line). When a penalty is refused, the down is not replayed, so the original second down now becomes third down. If the Bears decline, it would be third down and 2. It might be better for them to have a second down (two more chances to make a first down) and 4 yards to go rather than a third down (one more chance) and 2 yards to go. So, in this case, it may be advisable for Chicago to accept the penalty for a second down and 4.

Is this beginning to make sense? I hope so. Let's try another.

The New York Jets have a second down and 7 from their own 27-yard line. The quarterback completes a short pass for a gain of 5 yards. Now they are facing a third down and 2. However, during this play, one of the Jets' offensive linemen is guilty of holding, resulting in a 10-yard penalty. Their opponents, the Dallas Cowboys, have the option of accepting or declining the penalty. If Dallas accepts the penalty, what happens?

If the penalty is accepted, the penalty yardage (10) is enforced and the down is replayed. The Jets would still have a second down, but instead of 7 yards to go, it would be 17 (7 yards + 10 yards for the penalty). If Dallas accepts the penalty, then the Jets would have a second down and 17. If Dallas chooses to decline the penalty, what would the situation be? The play (gain of 5 yards) would be accepted and the down would not be replayed. It would become third down and 2 yards to go for the Jets, just as if the penalty never occurred.

One final example:

The Cleveland Browns have a first down and 10 yards to go and gain 9 yards on a sweep. Their opponents, the Tampa Bay Buccaneers, are guilty of having 12 men on the field (instead of the allowed 11) and are penalized 5 yards. If the Browns accept the penalty, the next play becomes first down and 5 yards to go. If they refuse the penalty, it becomes second down and 1 yard to go (10 yards minus 9 yards gained = 1 yard). If they refuse the penalty of 5 yards and accept the play, they get to "keep" the 9 yards they gained on the play. In this case, it would be best then if the Browns declined the penalty, since they would then need only 1 yard for a new first down.

Let's review.

Accepting the Penalty

- The officiating crew moves the guilty team backwards. If a play was in progress when the foul was committed, the play does not count.

- The same down is replayed.

Declining the Penalty

- The non-guilty team refuses the penalty yards.

- The ball is left at the spot where the previous play ended.

- The downs proceed as if no penalty were involved. The down is *not* replayed.

Generally, teams make decisions based on the amount of yardage gained on the play. In other words, if a team gains more yardage during a play than the penalty would give it, it usually accepts the play and refuses the penalty.

In most instances, teams choose to accept penalties and the downs are replayed. However, you will often see defensive teams decline a penalty when the offensive team commits a foul on third down play. Why? Most times defensive teams will decline penalties on third down because, in declining, they are preventing a third down from being replayed, in a sense giving the offense an extra chance to gain yardage sufficient for a first down. By declining, the defense is forcing the offense into a fourth down situation – the last chance for them to gain first down yardage. Fourth down situations often result in the offense having to give the ball over to the defense by punting.

Half the Distance to the Goal

You may wonder what happens if a team is assessed a penalty when it is deep in its own territory, near its own goal line. The rules state that if the yardage gained as a result of a penalty would advance the football more than half the distance to the fouling team's goal line, then the football is placed halfway between the goal line and the spot where the previous play ended.

If the Oakland Raiders commit a foul on their own 4-yard line, for example, how is a 5-yard penalty marked off against them? Remember, there are only 4 yards of playing space between the line of scrimmage and the Raiders' goal line, so even a 5-yard penalty could not be assessed in the conventional way. So how are the Raiders penalized?

The referee follows this sequence when assessing penalties near the guilty team's goal line:

1. First, he calculates the distance between the line of scrimmage and the goal line. In this case, 4 yards minus 0 yards (goal line) = 4 yards.

2. Then, he divides that number of yards by 2. 4 divided by 2 = 2 yards.

Two yards, then, is the amount of the penalty to be assessed in this case. Therefore, the ball would be moved from the Oakland 4-yard line back to the 2-yard line.

Keep in mind that although the **half the distance to the goal** rule can be enforced on succeeding plays, which can bring the team committing the fouls nearer and nearer to its own end zone, a touchdown can never be scored as a result of a penalty. If, however, a referee decides that an unfair act has been committed and a team has been deprived of a touchdown (to illustrate an unfair act and touchdown deprivation, the *NFL Digest of Rules* uses the example of an opposing player coming off the bench from the sidelines and tackling a runner apparently on his way to score a touchdown), the referee would rule that a touchdown had been scored as a result of the penalty.

Now that you have undergone a crash course in penalties, take a look at some of the most common penalty signals you'll see during a game. Although there are 48 different penalties that can be called during a game, I have included the most common ones here. The foul and its definition, and the appropriate penalty for the infraction are on the left, and an illustration of the officials' signals for each foul are at the right.

Penalties in football can be very difficult to understand, especially if you are a newcomer to the game. As you watch games, try to familiarize yourself with some of the most common signals. At this point, however, it is most important that you understand:

- The significance of the yellow flag being thrown.

- The team which commits a foul gets penalized in some way.

- The penalty can involve a loss of down, an automatic first down, a loss of yardage, or some combination, depending upon the severity of the infraction.

Penalties are indeed an important part of the game of football; they have been known to influence the game's momentum and, to a large degree, its results. So, keep a sharp eye on the referee and that yellow cloth. At the beginning, don't try to figure out the yardage and options involved with the penalties; the rulings can get very complicated. If you concentrate too intently on the calculations, it may ruin your interest and fun in watching the game. Let the officials do all the numbers work for you; that's what the NFL pays them to do! Watch the referee and his signals and listen to his explanations and those of your announcers. Soon you'll get to know exactly why fans get excited when they see a flag on the play.

Delay of game - If either team fails to be ready for play during a specified time limit. Also the signal for illegal substitution or too many time outs.
Penalty: Five yards

 Folded arms

False Start - An offensive player charges or moves after assuming a set position before the ball is snapped and the play begins. Also the signal for illegal formation on the offense, a kickoff, out of bounds, or kick out of bounds.
Penalty: Five yards

 Forearms rotated over and over in front of body

Illegal Motion - Movement of an offensive backfield player or the forward movement of the man in motion before the ball is snapped.
Penalty: Five yards

 Horizontal arc with one hand

Intentional Grounding - When the quarterback deliberately throws an incomplete pass in order to avoid being tackled ("sacked") behind the line of scrimmage.
Penalty: Loss of down and ten yards

 Parallel arms waved in a diagonal plane across body, followed by loss of down signal

Illegally Passing or Handing the Ball Forward - When the passer throws or hands off the ball from beyond, not behind, the line of scrimmage.
Penalty: Loss of down and five yards

 One hand placed behind back followed by loss of down signal

136

Pass Interference - Receiver interferes with a defensive back's ability to defend against a pass completion.
Penalty: Ten yards

Hands open and extended forward from shoulder with hands vertical

Ineligible Receiver Downfield - An offensive player who is not designated as an eligible receiver (i.e., a lineman) should not be downfield. Also the signal for ineligible member of kicking team downfield.
Penalty: Ten yards

Right hand touching top of cap

Personal Foul - A player commits an act involving illegal hitting or using unnecessary force against an opposing player.
Penalty: Fifteen yards

One wrist striking the other above head

Clipping - Running into or tackling the back of the legs of an opponent other than the player in possession of the football.
Penalty: Fifteen yards

Personal foul signal followed by hand striking back of calf

Roughing the Kicker - Tackling or running into the kicker in a violent manner.
Penalty: Fifteen yards plus an automatic first down
Running into the kicker -
Penalty: Five yards

Personal foul signal followed by swinging leg

Roughing the Passer - Running into or tackling the quarterback after the ball has left his hand.
Penalty: Fifteen yards plus an automatic first down

Personal foul signal followed by raised arm swinging forward

Holding - Illegal use of the hands while blocking a defensive player.
Penalty: Ten yards

 Grasping one wrist, the fist clenched in front of chest

Offside/Encroachment - When any part of the player's body is beyond the line of scrimmage before the ball has been snapped.
Penalty: Five yards

 Hands on hips

Grasping Opponent's Face Mask - When a player grasps, twists, turns or pulls an opponent by the face mask.
Penalty: Fifteen yards (if grasp was intentional)
Penalty: Five yards (if grasp was unintentional)

 Personal foul signal followed by face masking signal

Unsportsmanlike Conduct - Any act that is considered to be contrary to the principles of sportsmanship.
Penalty: Fifteen yards

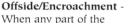 Arms outstretched and palms facing down

Tripping - A player deliberately extends his foot, causing an opposing player to stumble or fall.
Penalty: Ten yards

 Right foot in back of left heel

Invalid Fair Catch Signal -
Failure of the kick receiver to
give a proper fair catch signal.
Penalty: Five yards

One hand waved
above head

Defensive Holding - A
defensive player holds an
opposing player other than the
ball carrier.
Penalty: Five yards plus an
automatic first down

Grabs one wrist,
the fist clenched in
front of chest

**Illegal Use of Hands, Arms
or Body** - Player uses his
hands or arms illegally to
obstruct an opponent.
Penalty: Five yards plus an
automatic first down

Grasping one wrist
having the hand
open and facing
forward in front of
chest

Player Ejected - A player
commits a flagrant foul and is
ejected from the game.

Ejection signal,
clenched fist with
thumbs upward

☑ CHAPTER 10 CHECKLIST
THINGS TO REMEMBER

- Penalty – accept or decline (refuse)
- Referee makes all signals to teams, coaching staff and fans
- Recognize signals for:

personal foul	holding
false start	pass interference
delay of game	roughing the kicker
roughing the passer	clipping
unsportsmanlike conduct	

TERMS TO KNOW

accept	flag on the play
automatic first down	half the distance to the goal
decline	offsetting penalties

 **EXTRA POINTS: DID YOU KNOW?**

- **The Official National Football League 1992 Record and Fact Book** reports that more penalties (for two teams) were assessed in a game between the Cleveland Browns and the Chicago Bears on November 25, 1951, than in any other game in NFL history. The Browns were penalized 21 times for 209 yards while the Bears had 16 penalty flags thrown their way for 165 yards (total: 37 penalties for 374 yards).

CHAPTER 11

PUTTING IT ALL TOGETHER: THE BIG PICTURE

"What's it called when one of the participants propels an oblong pigskin through the enlarged H?" - Jean S. (1992)

Now that we have gone through separate discussions of some basic elements of the game of football, let's see how well you can combine them and apply what you've learned.

This chapter takes you step-by-step through a series of plays taken from a hypothetical football game played between the New Orleans Saints and the Miami Dolphins.

Kickoff

Since Miami has won the coin toss and has elected to receive, the football game begins with a kickoff by the Saints (the kicking team) to the Dolphins (the receiving team). The kickoff takes place on the Saints' 30-yard line between the inbound lines. Once Miami catches the ball, it will try to advance it in the direction of the Saints' goal line.

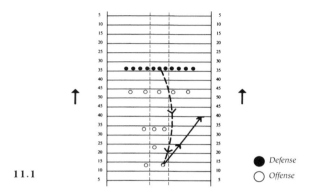

11.1

● Defense
○ Offense

Kickoff Return

The Dolphins' kick returner catches the ball on his own 15-yard line and runs with it upfield for 25 yards. (See Diagram 11.1) Once he is tackled and the ball is whistled dead, Miami substitutes players and begins a series of offensive plays from that spot on the field.

First Down and 10

The Miami offense, led by the quarterback, breaks out of the huddle and lines up at its own 40-yard line, the spot where the previous play ended. It has four plays or downs in which to gain 10 yards (to the 50-yard line). Remember, it can do this advancing of the ball through running or passing plays. On the first play, the quarterback hands off the ball to his running back, who runs forward to the 44-yard line for a gain of 4 yards (see Diagram 11.2).

Since Miami had a first down and 10 and gained 4 yards, its next play or down becomes second down and 6 yards to go.

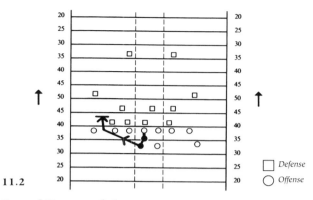

11.2

Defense □
Offense ○

Second Down and 6

On this play, the quarterback passes to one of his wide receivers. New Orleans tackles the receiver at the 49-yard line for a gain of 5 yards (see Diagram 11.3).

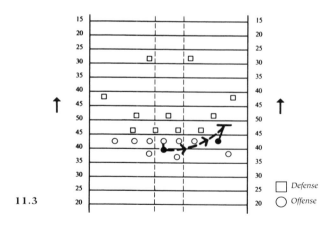

11.3

Defense □
Offense ○

Since the receiver gained 5 yards, the next play becomes third down and 1 to go. The Dolphins need to gain one more yard to get to the 50-yard line to gain a total of 10 yards. They get to keep the football, have a new first down, and have four more plays.

Third Down and 1

On this play, the quarterback hands off to his fullback who attempts to run straight ahead. He gets only to the line of scrimmage (the 49-yard line) before he is tackled by one of the Saints' defensive linemen. Therefore, there is no gain on this play. (See Diagram 11.4).

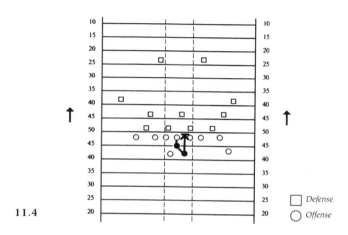

11.4

Since the Dolphins needed to gain 1 yard to the 50-yard line for a first down but failed to do so, it's now fourth down and 1 (1 yard minus 0 yards gained = 1 yard).

Fourth Down and 1

Since this is the fourth play and the Dolphins have not gained the 10 yards necessary for a new first down, they must make a decision. They have several options to consider:

- They can attempt to gain the 1 yard by running or passing.
- They can attempt to kick a field goal.
- They can kick (punt) the ball to the Saints.

If Miami's attempt to gain the one yard is unsuccessful, it must turn the ball over to New Orleans "on downs" at the point where the ball was spotted at the end of the fourth down play. It is unlikely that Miami would try a field goal from its own territory, since field goals are usually attempted only from within the opponent's 35-yard line.

The Dolphins do not want to take a chance of having New Orleans take possession of the ball on their own 49-yard line, by either missing a field goal or failing to gain 1 yard, so they choose to punt the ball to the Saints, whose punt returners are waiting at the other end of the field. At this time two special teams take the field: the punting team of the Dolphins and the punt return team of the Saints.

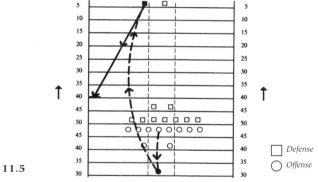

11.5

Defense

Offense

The Miami punter lines up 15 yards behind the line of scrimmage to await the snap from the center. After shouting the cadence, the punter takes the snap from the center and punts the ball to the Saints, who, on this play, make up the punt return team. The Saints' punt returner catches the ball on his own 5-yard line and runs upfield for a nice gain of 35 yards. (See Diagram 11.5) The two special teams leave the field, and the Saints' offense and the Miami defense enter the game. The Saints' offense takes over and begins its series of plays from its own 40-yard line with a first down and 10.

145

First Down and 10

The offense lines up on its own 40-yard line. The quarterback sees the alignment the defense is using and decides to change the play. He therefore calls an audible at the line of scrimmage, then passes to his wide receiver who gains 10 yards on the play before being stopped by the left cornerback. Since the Saints gained the 10 yards necessary for a new first down, it is now first down and 10 from midfield, the 50-yard line. (See Diagram 11.6)

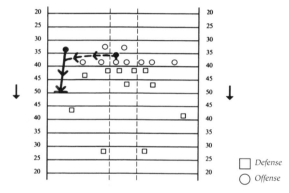

11.6

First and 10

The quarterback drops back into the pocket to pass. He is under pressure from the defense, tries to scramble, but gets sacked behind the line of scrimmage, back to his own 42-yard line for an 8-yard loss. Since there is a loss on the play, New Orleans must add that loss in yardage to the original 10 yards they needed to gain for a first down (10 yards plus the 8 yards lost = 18 yards). Therefore, the next play becomes second and 18.

Second Down and 18

The quarterback hands the football off to the running back who breaks a couple of tackles, gets in the clear, runs upfield for 58 yards, crosses Miami's goal line, and scores a touchdown worth 6 points. (See Diagram 11.7)

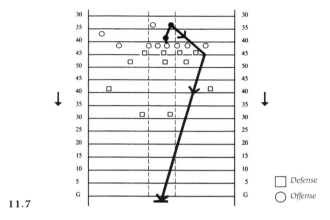

Defense
Offense

The extra point unit comes onto the field and spots the ball on the Miami 2-yard line. The ball is snapped to the holder, who puts it down and holds it upright for the kicker. The kicker then boots it through the uprights for a 1-point score. The scoring drive of the Saints involves three plays for 60 yards and takes three minutes and 45 seconds (3:45) to complete. The score is New Orleans 7, Miami 0. Since New Orleans has scored, it must now give the ball back to Miami.

Kickoff

The Saints' kickoff team takes the field. The kicker kicks the ball high; it is caught on the Miami 25-yard line by the Dolphins' deep man (the kick returner) who brings it upfield 21 yards before he is downed on his own 46-yard line. The Miami offense then starts from that spot with a first down and 10.

First Down and 10

The quarterback throws a quick screen pass to one of his running backs for a gain of 3 yards. (See Diagram 11.8) It's now second down and 7 from the 49.

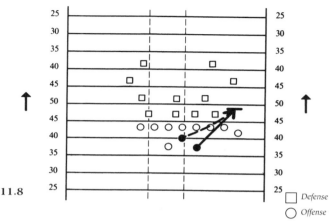

11.8

Defense □

Offense ○

Second Down and 7

The quarterback pitches out to his halfback, who cuts back over the middle for a gain of 5 into New Orleans' territory, to the Saints' 46-yard line. The next play becomes third down and 2. The Miami quarterback throws a quick sideline pass to one of his receivers for a gain of 3, enough for a first down. The next play is first and 10 from the 43 of New Orleans.

First Down and 10

The quarterback lines up in a "shot gun" formation several yards behind the center, which indicates he may pass. He throws a short sideline pass to his tight end, who rumbles for 12 yards before being brought down at the New Orleans 31-yard line. (See Diagram 11.9)

Since the Dolphins gained the 10 yards necessary for a new first down, it is once again first down and 10.

First Down and 10

On this play, the fullback takes the handoff, sweeps around the right side and is driven out of bounds after a 5-yard gain.

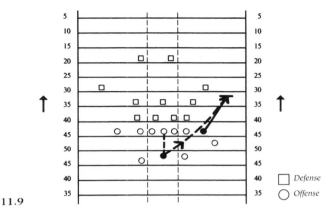

11.9

Second Down and 5

The ball is on the 26; the quarterback drops back to pass, but the Saints sack him back on the 33-yard line for a loss of 7 yards. (See Diagram 11.10) Remember, since there was a loss, add that loss to the yardage needed from the previous play (7 yard loss + 5 yards = 12 yards). Second down and 5 yards to go now becomes third down and 12.

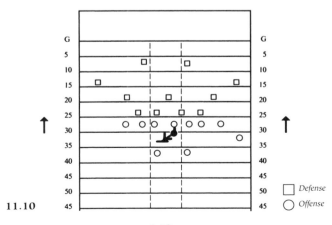

11.10

149

Third Down and 12

The quarterback passes to his wide receiver for a gain of 10 yards to the 23-yard line. Since Miami made only 10 yards, but needed 12 yards for a first down, it is now fourth down and 2.

Fourth Down and 2

Since the Dolphins are well inside the Saints' territory (the 23-yard line), they elect to attempt a field goal. Remember that since 17 yards are added to the distance between the line of scrimmage (the 23-yard line) and the opponents' goal line, this is a 40-yard field goal attempt. The center snaps the ball to the teammate holder, who places the ball down on the ground. The kicker kicks the ball through the uprights for a field goal worth 3 points. (See Diagram 11.11)

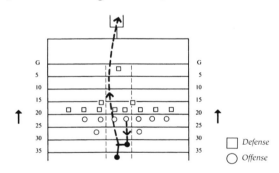

11.11

Now the score is New Orleans 7, Miami 3. Since the Dolphins just scored, they must now kick off to the Saints.

This action involving various combinations of plays, scoring, and changes in possession of the football, continues until 60 minutes of regulation playing time have expired.

Although there are literally dozens of plays, strategies and formations that are used during a football game, the diagrams included here show only a few examples. By referring to Diagrams 11.1 - 11.11. you can track the step-by-step progress of a team's scoring drive. I hope this chapter helped you to integrate the facts, rules, and terms you learned in previous chapters and were able to apply them in this actual game situation.

☑ CHAPTER 11 CHECKLIST
THINGS TO REMEMBER

- After a team scores a safety or either scores (or misses) a field goal or an extra point, it must kick the ball to its opponent.

- When calculating the distance of a field goal, first figure out the distance between the line of scrimmage and the opponent's goal line. Then add 17 yards to that number. That number is the distance of the field goal.

EXTRA POINTS: DID YOU KNOW?

According to USA Today research (January 1994), the National Football League has increased the payments for both the winners and losers of the Super Bowl game. The winners of Super Bowl XXVIII on January 30, 1994, the Dallas Cowboys, received $38,000 per player (an increase of 5.6% over the old payment of $36,000) while the losing team, the Buffalo Bills, received $23,500 per player (an increase of 30.6% over the old payment of $18,000).

CHAPTER 12

FOOTBALL BY THE NUMBERS

"I need some help in figuring this stuff out. This looks like something the ancient Egyptians might have written." - John L. (1989)

As I stated in the beginning of this book, the best way to learn any new material is to expose yourself to it through various formats. Now that you have read most of this book and, hopefully, have watched a game or two, how can you reinforce what you have learned so that you can intelligently discuss the game? This chapter acquaints you with various statistics, records, and charts that you can use as supplemental materials to help you build upon what you have already learned. We'll discuss statistics that are found in NFL Standings, NFL Playoffs, box scores, the quarterback rating system, takeaways, giveaways and turnover ratios.

One easy way to learn new material is to rely on the media. Since the world of sports, particularly professional football, enjoys phenomenal popularity, there is certainly no lack of football information reported in the newspaper, sports magazines, or on the radio and television.

FINAL NFL STANDINGS
1994-95
American Conference
EAST

	W	L	T	Pct	PF	PA	Home	Away	AFC	NFC	Div
Miami	10	6	0	.625	389	327	6-2-0	4-4-0	8-4-0	2-2-0	5-3-0
New England	10	6	0	.625	351	312	5-3-0	5-3-0	6-6-0	4-0-0	4-4-0
Indianapolis	8	8	0	.500	307	320	5-3-0	3-5-0	8-6-0	0-2-0	4-4-0
Buffalo	7	9	0	.438	340	356	4-4-0	3-5-0	6-6-0	1-3-0	3-5-0
NY Jets	6	10	0	.375	264	320	4-4-0	2-6-0	5-7-0	1-3-0	4-4-0

CENTRAL

	W	L	T	Pct	PF	PA	Home	Away	AFC	NFC	Div
Pittsburgh	12	4	0	.750	316	234	7-1-0	5-3-0	10-2-0	2-2-0	6-0-0
Cleveland	11	5	0	.688	340	204	6-2-0	5-3-0	8-4-0	3-1-0	4-2-0
Cincinnati	3	13	0	.188	276	406	2-6-0	1-7-0	2-10-0	1-3-0	1-5-0
Houston	2	14	0	.125	226	352	2-6-0	0-8-0	2-10-0	0-4-0	1-5-0

WEST

	W	L	T	Pct	PF	PA	Home	Away	AFC	NFC	Div
San Diego	11	5	0	.688	381	306	5-3-0	6-2-0	9-3-0	2-2-0	6-2-0
Kansas City	9	7	0	.563	319	298	5-3-0	4-4-0	6-6-0	3-1-0	4-4-0
LA Raiders	9	7	0	.438	303	327	4-4-0	5-3-0	6-6-0	3-1-0	4-4-0
Denver	7	9	0	.438	347	396	4-4-0	3-5-0	6-6-0	1-3-0	4-4-0
Seattle	6	10	0	.375	287	323	3-5-0	3-5-0	4-10-0	2-0-0	2-6-0

National Conference
EAST

	W	L	T	Pct	PF	PA	Home	Away	AFC	NFC	Div
Dallas	12	4	0	.750	414	248	6-2-0	6-2-0	3-1-0	9-3-0	7-1-0
NY Giants	9	7	0	.563	279	305	4-4-0	5-3-0	3-1-0	6-6-0	6-2-0
Arizona	8	8	0	.500	235	267	5-3-0	3-5-0	3-1-0	5-7-0	4-4-0
Philadelphia	7	9	0	.438	308	308	5-3-0	2-6-0	1-3-0	6-6-0	3-5-0
Washington	3	13	0	.188	320	412	0-8-0	3-5-0	1-1-0	2-12-0	0-8-0

CENTRAL

	W	L	T	Pct	PF	PA	Home	Away	AFC	NFC	Div
Minnesota	10	6	0	.600	356	314	6-2-0	4-4-0	2-2-0	8-4-0	5-3-0
Green Bay	9	7	0	.563	382	287	7-1-0	2-6-0	1-3-0	8-4-0	6-2-0
Detroit	9	7	0	.563	357	342	6-2-0	3-5-0	2-2-0	7-5-0	4-4-0
Chicago	9	7	0	.563	271	307	5-3-0	4-4-0	3-1-0	6-6-0	3-5-0
Tampa Bay	6	10	0	.375	251	351	4-4-0	2-6-0	1-1-0	5-9-0	2-6-0

WEST

	W	L	T	Pct	PF	PA	Home	Away	AFC	NFC	Div
San Francisco	13	3	0	.813	505	286	7-1-0	6-2-0	3-1-0	10-2-0	6-0-0
New Orleans	7	9	0	.438	348	407	3-5-0	4-4-0	1-3-0	6-6-0	4-8-0
Atlanta	7	9	0	.438	313	389	5-3-0	2-6-0	1-3-0	6-6-0	2-4-0
LA Rams	4	12	0	.250	286	365	3-5-0	1-7-0	2-2-0	6-6-0	2-4-0

12.1 NFL STANDINGS

153

An excellent way to reinforce any material that you have learned is by reading the sports pages of your local newspaper; Monday's edition is particularly helpful. Try to become familiar with the various types of statistics such as the chart called the **NFL Standings** (12.1).

Although it looks confusing, the NFL Standings are actually easy to interpret once you know what all the categories, symbols, and numbers mean.

The standings, like most NFL records, are divided into two parts: the **American Football Conference (AFC)** and the **National Football Conference (NFC)**. Each conference standings are further sub-divided by division: **East**, **Central**, and **West**.

The standings give an overall picture of how each team performed individually during the 16-game season and how its record compared with the other teams in the league. To make the explanation of the standings easy, we'll move from left to right across the top of the chart.

On the extreme left, all the teams are listed according to their Won-Lost-Tied record. The team that has the best Won-Lost-Tied record is at the top, while the team with the worst record is at the bottom. The symbols across the top of the chart are as follows:

W Number of Wins

L Number of Losses

T Number of Ties

Pct Percentage of games the team won. To calculate a team's percentage, divide the number of wins (W) by the total number of games played (16)

PF Points For - The total number of points a team scored

PA Points Against/Points Allowed - The total number of points scored against a team

So, for example, we can tell that in 1994, the San Francisco 49ers (NFC West) had the best record with 13 wins and 3 losses, and had the winningest percentage. The 49ers were followed closely by the Pittsburgh Steelers (AFC Central) and Dallas Cowboys (NFC East) with records of 12-4-0. We can also see that the Houston Oilers (AFC Central) were in the unenviable position of winning the fewest number of games (2). The San Francisco 49ers (NFC West) scored the most points (505), while Houston scored the fewest (226). The Cleveland Browns had the fewest number of points scored against them (204), while the Washington Redskins gave up the most (412).

PF and PA

What do the PF and PA tell you about a team? A high PF indicates that a team has a good offense, capable of scoring a lot of points. A high PA tells you that a team does not have a very good defense and allows a lot of points to be scored against it. On the other hand, a low PA indicates that a team has a good defense and does not give up many points.

The higher the PF for a team and the lower its PA, the better its record tends to be. The smaller the discrepancy between the PF and the PA, the worse the record is. If you see a team that has given up approximately the same number of points (PA) as it has scored (PF), it tends to have its percentage close to .500, or in other words, has the same or close to the same number of wins as losses.

The next elements across the top of the standings chart are as follows: **Home, Away, AFC, NFC**, and **Division (Div.)**. Under each of these columns you will see a series of three numbers, which again refers to the team's number of wins, losses and ties. Remember that each team plays eight games on its home field and eight games away on its opponents' fields.

Home	Record of the team when it plays on its home field.
Away	Record of the team when it plays away or "**on the road.**"
AFC	Record of a particular team against teams from the American Football Conference.
NFC	Record of a particular team against teams from the National Football Conference.
Div.	Record of a team against teams within the same division.

What does this tell us about particular teams? The Pittsburgh Steelers, Green Bay Packers and San Francisco 49ers had almost perfect records (7-1-0) at home, while the Washington Redskins did not win any games (0-8-0). You can tell that the Dallas Cowboys, the San Diego Chargers, and the San Francisco 49ers were all good road teams (6-2-0), but the Houston Oilers were poor (0-8-0). Within their divisions, San Francisco and Pittsburgh both had perfect records (6-0-0), while other teams such as the Washington Redskins (0-8-0) and the Cincinnati Bengals (1-5-0) did not play well against their divisional opponents.

As you now can see, the NFL Standings contain a lot of useful information. If you have a favorite team, you can follow its progress by checking the standings each week. Most newspapers print the standings every day during the football season.

NFL PLAYOFFS

One of the most complicated aspects of the game of professional football involves the NFL Playoff system. I honestly believe that the only people who really understand this system are Paul Tagliabue, the Commissioner of the National Football League; Jerry Seeman, Director of NFL Officiating; and maybe a couple of other individuals who happen to have advanced degrees in statistical mathematics. For the rest of us, it is an annual nightmare trying to figure out exactly how the system picks the teams that make it to the playoffs.

Professional sports differ greatly in the way their playoff systems are organized and the number of playoff games played. For example, while the maximum total number of playoff games among all teams in professional basketball is 89, and for major league baseball, 41, the maximum number of playoff games for professional football is only 11. Another difference among the sports involves the playoff games themselves; unlike other sports, such as basketball, baseball, and hockey, in which teams advance to the next round of the post-season play by winning a certain number of games (i.e., first team to win three games out of five or four games out of seven, as in baseball's World Series), professional football's playoffs involve one and only one game. The **single elimination** system in football is quite simple: if you win the game, you advance; if you lose, your season is over. No second chances in football.

The NFL decided to change to a 17-week, 16-game schedule with one bye for the 1994-95 season. With this in mind, I will briefly explain the workings of the NFL playoff system.

How Teams Are Selected For The Playoffs

At the end of the regular season (after 16 games), the NFL takes a look at all the Won-Lost-Tied records and identifies those teams with the best records as the ones that will advance to the playoffs.

You will recall that there are two conferences that make up the National Football League: the American Football Conference (AFC) and the National Football Conference (NFC). Each conference is then subdivided into three divisions: East, Central and West. With this information, you are now able to begin to identify the teams selected for the playoffs.

The first six teams selected are those that have the best records outright in their division. Suppose, however, that more than one team in a division have identical

Won-Lost-Tied records. What happens then? Which team is the division champion?

There is a set of **tie breaker** procedures that the NFL uses in the selection process when potential playoff teams with identical records are competing for a limited number of playoff slots. They are compared to each other by using several variables in the following order:

1. Games against each other (best Won-Lost-Tied percentage)

2. Best division record (best Won-Lost-Tied record in games within the division)

3. Best conference record (best Won-Lost-Tied record within the conference)

4. Same team performance (how each team fared against the same opponents)

5. Most net points in division games (total number of points scored minus the number of points it allowed to be scored against it)

6. Most net points in all games

7. How difficult the teams' schedules were (how well-rated or poorly-rated their opponents were)

8. Most net touchdowns in all games (total number of touchdowns a team scores minus the number it allowed opposing teams to score)

9. Coin toss

Now that you have briefly familiarized yourself with the playoff team selection process, let's see who made the 1995 playoffs. By looking at the NFL Standings (page 153), we can see that the following teams were Division champions for the 1994-95 season:

AFC East	Miami Dolphins	10-6-0
AFC Central	Pittsburgh Steelers	12-4-0
AFC West	San Diego Chargers	11-5-0
NFC East	Dallas Cowboys	12-4-0

158

| **NFC Central** | Minnesota Vikings 10-6-0 |
| **NFC West** | San Francisco 49ers 13-3-0 |

After the six divisional champs have been selected, the rest of the teams compete for six **wild card** slots, three from each conference.

Wild cards are those three teams which have the best second place records in each conference. Refer to the standings once again, and you can tell that the six wild card teams for the 1994-95 season were:

AFC	Kansas City Chiefs 9-7-0
AFC	Cleveland Browns 11-5-0
AFC	New England Patriots 10-6-0
NFC	Detroit Lions 9-7-0
NFC	Chicago Bears 9-7-0
NFC	Green Bay Packers 9-7-0

Since an even number of teams is necessary for pairing during post-season play, the division champion with the worst record in each conference must play against one of the wild card teams. The division champions with the four best records do not play in the first round of the playoffs; they have a bye or an off week and do not have to play until the second round of the playoffs.

Although the NFL Playoff system can be extremely complicated, the tricky part only involves the initial selection of all the playoff teams. I believe, however, that for purposes of this discussion, it is most important that you become familiar with terms such as **wild card**, **divisional**, and **conference rounds**, and that you come to understand how each round relates to the Super Bowl game.

Journey to the Super Bowl

To make the playoff picture as clear as possible, I have included a chart (12.2) detailing the way NFL teams make their way through the playoff rounds, using the 1994-95 playoffs as an illustration.

Once all the teams have been selected for participation in the playoffs, they begin play using the following format:

First Round Playoff Games

A - AFC Wild Card vs. AFC Division Champ

B - NFC Wild Card vs. NFC Wild Card

C - AFC Wild Card vs. AFC Wild Card

D - NFC Wild Card vs. NFC Division Champ

Divisional Playoff Games

E - Winner of the game between two AFC Wild Cards vs. AFC Division Champ

F - Winner of game between two NFC Wild Cards vs. NFC Division Champ

G - Winner of game between AFC Wild Card and AFC Division Champ vs. AFC Division Champ

H - Winner of game between NFC Wild Card and NFC Division Champ vs. NFC Division Champ

Conference Championship Games

I - Winner of the first AFC Divisional Playoff game vs. the winner of the second AFC Divisional playoff game

J - Winner of the first NFC Divisional Playoff game vs. the winner of the second NFC Divisional Playoff game

Super Bowl Game

K - Winner of the AFC Conference Championship game vs. the winner of the NFC Conference Championship game

NFL PLAYOFFS 1994 - 95

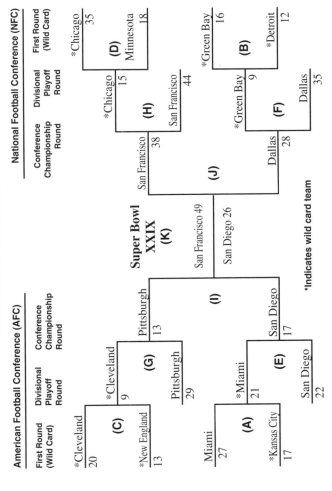

12.2 1994-95 PLAYOFFS

Now that you are somewhat familiar with the format of the playoff system, which teams actually advanced through the 1994-95 playoff rounds? To make this easier to understand, please refer to Diagram 13.2 and the letters A through K. The following games took place between December 1994 and January 1995.

First Round Playoff Games

A - Miami Dolphins vs. Kansas City Chiefs

B - Green Bay Packers vs. Detroit Lions

C - Cleveland Browns vs. New England Patriots

D - Chicago Bears vs. Minnesota Vikings

Divisional Playoff Games

As you can tell from the chart, both the Miami Dolphins (Game A) and the Cleveland Browns (Game C) from the AFC, and the Green Bay Packers (Game B) and the Chicago Bears (Game D) from the NFC won their wild card games and moved to the second playoff round, also known as the divisional playoff or conference semi-final round.

E - San Diego Chargers vs. Miami Dolphins

F - Green Bay Packers vs. Dallas Cowboys

G - Pittsburgh Steelers vs. Cleveland Browns

H - San Francisco 49ers vs. Chicago Bears

In the Divisional Games E, F, G and H, four teams emerged victorious and took the next step toward the Super Bowl: Pittsburgh Steelers and San Diego Chargers for the AFC, and the San Francisco 49ers and Dallas Cowboys for the NFC.

Conference Championship Games

I - San Diego Chargers vs. Pittsburgh Steelers

J - San Francisco 49ers vs. Dallas Cowboys

The third round of the playoffs determines which teams will be conference champions, or in other words, which teams will represent their respective conference in the Super Bowl. (Remember in Chapter 1 you read that the Super Bowl is the game played between the champion of the AFC and the champion of the NFC.)

Once again, by looking at the chart you can tell which two teams won their conference championship game and, as a result, advanced to the final round. The San Diego Chargers (Game I) became AFC Champions, while the San Francisco 49ers (Game J), became the NFC Champions.

Super Bowl Game

K - San Diego Chargers (AFC) vs. San Francisco 49ers (NFC)

In the final game (Game K), the Super Bowl, the culmination of an entire football season involving a lot of hard work, blood, sweat, and tears, the San Francisco 49ers (NFC) won the Super Bowl by soundly defeating the San Diego Chargers by a score of 49-26.

I hope this discussion helped you understand the NFL Playoff system so that when January comes around and you find yourself in the midst of playoff and pre-Super Bowl hysteria, you'll know what all the hoopla is about.

Miscellaneous Statistics

In addition to statistics found in the newspaper, you can find all sorts of interesting charts and records in sports magazines, on football trading cards, and even on your television screen during a game. The information can be related to either an individual player or a team's performance. Since you will come across some important abbreviations and categories, I have included the most common ones here (12.3). Once you become familiar with them, you will find football information easy to follow,

Abbrev./Term	Meaning
All Purpose	Category made by adding rushing, receiving and kick/punt return yardage together.
ATT	Attempts – The number of times a quarterback tries to pass or the number of times a player/team runs with the ball, or the number of times a player/team tries a field goal.
AVG	Average – May be used to refer to the yardage in - average gain per reception (WR/TE)* - average length of a punt (P)* - average gain per carry (RB)* - average punt/kick return (PR)/KR* - average gain per completion (QB)*
Car	Carries – The number of times a player carries the ball in a running play
COMP	Completions – Number of passes completed (QB)*
FC	Fair Catch (PK/KR)*
FG	Field Goals Made (PK/K)*
FGA	Field Goals Attempted (PK/K)*
FUM	Fumbles – The number of fumbles recovered (takeaways) or the number of fumbles lost (giveaways)
GM	Game
INT	Interceptions – The number of interceptions made (takeaways) or interceptions given up (giveaways)
Long	Longest gain or distance in a particular category relating to passing, rushing or kicking. If you see a "t" next to the yardage under Long, it means that the play resulted in a touchdown.
L	Losses
Net. Diff.	Net Difference
No.	Number
PAT	Point After Touchdown
Pct.	Percentage – Percentages related to passing (completions divided by attempts) and third down efficiency (first downs converted divided by number of third down plays)
Pts.	Points
Rec.	Receptions
SAF	Safeties
TDM	Touchdowns (miscellaneous) – Refers to touchdowns made by interception returns, fumble recoveries, kick returns and punt returns.
TDP	Touchdowns scored by Passing
TDR	Touchdowns scored by Rushing (Running)
TDS	Touchdowns
T	Ties
TD	Touchdown
XP	Extra points made (PK/K)*
XPA	Extra points attempted (PK/K)*
YDS	Yards – Can be found under the categories of rushing, passing, kicking, or returns.

QB=Quarterback, WR=Wide Receiver, P=Punter, RB=Running Back, PR=Punt Returner, PK=Placekicker, K=Kicker

12.3 MISCELLANEOUS STATISTICS

whatever the source. In addition to these descriptions of the statistics and abbreviations, I have included the abbreviation of the player position(s) most closely associated with them.

Box Score/Game Summary

Another good source of information is the **box score**, also called **game summary**, which is a record of play of a football game and is usually found in the NFL section of the sports pages, often at the end of an article describing a particular game.

Like the standings, box scores are easy to read once you learn how to interpret them. Below is an actual box score taken from what I believe is one of the finest games I have ever watched, the 1990 NFC Championship game between the New York Giants and the San Francisco 49ers. The game was exciting down to the last few seconds when Matt Bahr, the Giants' placekicker, booted the Giants into the 1991 Super Bowl by kicking a 42-yard field goal with only seconds remaining on the clock. Look through this box score carefully; try to figure out what the statistics mean before I explain them to you.

1990 NFC Championship Game
Candlestick Park, San Francisco
January 20, 1991

I.　　　Score by Periods

	1	2	3	4	Total
NY	3	3	3	6	15
SF	3	3	7	0	13

II.　　　Scoring

a	b	c	d	e	f	g	h
SF-FG	Cofer	47	5:07	1st	Drive - 44 yd.	10 plays
NY-FG	Bahr	28	12:19	1st	Drive - 69 yd.	15 plays
NY-FG	Bahr	42	14:00	2nd	Drive - 56 yd.	14 plays
SF-FG	Cofer	35	14:57	2nd	Drive - 48 yd	7 plays
SF-TD	Taylor	61**	4:32	3rd	Drive - 61 yd.	1 play

** pass from Montana (Cofer kick)

a	b	c	d	e	f	g	h
NY-FG	Bahr	46	10:35	3rd	Drive - 49 yd.	10 plays
NY-FG	Bahr	38	9:13	4th	Drive - 41 yd.	8 plays
NY-FG	Bahr	42	15:00	4th	Drive - 33 yd.	7 plays

III.　　　Team Statistics

	New York	San Francisco
a. First Downs	20	13
Rushing	8	1
Passing	8	11
Penalty	4	1
b. Third Down Efficiency	6-15	1-8
c. Total Net Yards	311	240
Offensive Plays	68	41
Average gain per play	4.6 yds.	5.9 yds.
d. Net yards Rushing	152	39
Total Rushes	36	11
Avg. gain per rush	4.2	3.5

e. **Net Yards Passing**	159	201
Sacked - yards lost	3-17	3-14
Gross yards passing	176	215
f. **Passes**	15-29-0	19-27-0
Avg. gain per pass	5.0	6.7
g. **Punts**	3-41.3	5-40.0
Had blocked	0	0
h. **Total Return Yardage**	81	125
Punt returns	42	40
Kickoff returns	39	85
Interception returns	0	0
i. **Penalties - Yards**	5-45	9-63
j. **Fumbles - Lost**	0-0	3-1
k. **Time of Possession**	38:59	21:01
l. **Attendance:** 65,750		

IV. Individual Statistics

a. **Rushing NY** Anderson 20-67, Meggett 10-36, Reasons 1-30, Hostetler 3-11, Carthon 2-8 **SF** Craig 8-26, Montana 2-9, Rathman 1-4

b. **Passing NY** Hostetler 15-27-0-176, Meggett 0-1-0-0, Cavanaugh 0-1-0-0 **SF** Montana 18-26-0-190, Young 1-1-0-25

c. **Receiving NY** Ingram 5-82, Bavaro 5-54, Baker 2-22, Meggett 2-15, Anderson 1-3 **SF** Rice 5-54, Rathman 4-16, Jones 3-46, Craig 3-16, Taylor 2-75, Sherrard 2-8

d. **Kickoff Returns NY** Meggett 2-36, Cross 1-3, **SF** D. Carter 3-74, Tillman 1-11

e. **Punt Returns NY** Meggett 5-42, **SF** Taylor 2-40

f. **Interceptions** None

g. **Punting NY** Landeta 3-41.3, **SF** Helton 5-40.0

h. **Field Goals NY** Bahr 5-6 (missed 37) **SF** Cofer 2-2

i. **Sacks NY** Marshall 2, Howard 1/2, Taylor 1/2 **SF** Burt 1, Haley 1, Holt 1

12.4 Box Score

I. Score by Periods - Breakdown of the points each team scored by quarter and the total number of points scored in the game.

II. Scoring - This section gives an overview of the scoring specifics which occurred during the game. From left to right this scoring section lists:

a. Name of the team that scored

b. The type of score (touchdown, field goal, or safety)

c. Name of the person who scored the point(s)

d. Length of field goal or the touchdown yardage

e. Official time when the score occurred

f. Quarter in which the score occurred

g. Total number of yards in the scoring drive

h. Total number of plays in the scoring drive

III. Team Statistics

a. **First downs** – The number of first downs earned by each team during the game. First downs are classified as to how they were earned.
    Rushing – Earned on a running play.
    Passing – Earned on a passing play.
    Penalty – Earned as a result of penalties against the opponent. In this game, for example, the New York Giants earned 4 first downs as a result of penalties against their opponents, the San Francisco 49ers.

b. **Third down efficiency** – Refers to the number of times a team converted third down plays into first downs. The first number is the number of first downs, the second is the total number of third down plays. In this game, you can see that San Francisco converted only 1 out of 8 third down plays into first downs.

c. **Total net yards** – Total number of yards gained by both teams. This category also includes the number of **offensive plays** and the average number of yards gained per play.

d. **Net yards rushing** – Total number of yards gained on running plays.

   Total Rushes – Total number of times a team ran with the ball.

   Average gain per rush – Average number of yards gained per carry, or each time the team ran with the ball.

e. **Net yards passing** – Total number of yards gained on passing plays after losses have been subtracted.

   Sacked - Yards Lost – The total number of times a team's quarterback was sacked and the total number of yards lost as a result of these sacks.

   Gross yards passing – Total number of yards gained on passing plays before losses have been subtracted. The gross yardage is calculated by adding the net yards to the yards lost due to sacks.

f. **Passes** – This refers to the number of passes thrown during the game. The first number refers to the number of completions; the second number is the total number of pass attempts; the third number refers to the number of interceptions. You can tell by this box score, then, that the San Francisco 49ers completed 19 passes out of 27 attempts with no interceptions.

   Average gain per pass – The average number of yards gained per pass.

g. **Punts** – The total number of punts and the average distance each punt traveled.

   Had blocked – Number of blocked punts.

h. **Total Return Yardage** – The total number of yards gained in all returns (punt, kickoff and interceptions)

>   **Punt returns** – the yardage gained in punt returns

>   **Kickoff returns** – the yardage gained in kickoff returns

>   **Interception returns** – The yardage gained by players intercepting the ball.

i. **Penalties - Yards** – The number of penalties assessed to a team and the amount of penalty yardage assessed against it. In this game, for example, the Giants were penalized five times for 45 yards.

j. **Fumbles - Lost** – The number of times a team fumbled the ball. The first number refers to the total number of fumbles; the second to the number of fumbles lost or recovered by the opposing team.

k. **Time of Possession** – The number of minutes and seconds that each team had the ball. These two numbers should always add up to 60:00 minutes for a regulation game.

l. **Attendance** – The number of people attending the game.

IV. Individual Statistics

a. **Rushing** – Total number of yards gained by individual players. The team name is printed first, followed by the player's name, the number of times he carried the ball and the total number of yards he gained.

b. **Passing** – Performance by individual players. The team name first, player's name followed by number of pass completions, number of pass attempts, number of interceptions and total number of yards gained by passing.

c. **Receiving** – Performance by individual receivers. The team name, player's name, number of receptions and total number of yards gained through these receptions.

d. **Kickoff returns** – Performance by kick return specialists. The team name, player's name, number of kickoffs and the total number of yards gained on the kickoff return(s).

e. **Punt returns** – Performance by punt returners. The team name, player's name, number of punt returns and total number of yards gained on the punt return(s).

f. **Interceptions** – Individual players who intercepted. The team name, player's name, number of interceptions and the total number of yards gained on the interception return(s). In this game, there were no interceptions.

g. **Punting** – Performance by individual punters. The team name, player's name, number of punts, and the average distance of each punt.

h. **Field goals** – Performance by individual field goal kickers. The team name, player's name, number of successful field goals, number of field goal attempts and the distance of any missed field goal. The box score tells us that Matt Bahr of the New York Giants made five out of six field goals, missing only a 37-yarder.

i. **Sacks** – Performance of individuals who tackled or sacked the opposing quarterback behind the line of scrimmage. The team name, player's name, and total number of sacks. If two players sack a quarterback at the same time, each player is awarded a half sack.

Box scores provide a summary of useful information on every football game. They are especially valuable to those fans who have favorite teams and like to check on individual statistics and performances of key players.

Look for the box scores in the sports section; they usually follow the narrative summary of the game. As with most NFL information, the best source for box scores and the NFL Standings is Monday's newspaper (or Tuesday's after the Monday night game).

Quarterback Rating

On occasion, you may have run across a quarterback's name followed by a numerical rating, known as the **quarterback rating**.

The National Football League has a Passing Efficiency rating system, which is based on quarterback performance standards for percentage of passes completed, average gain per pass, percentage of passes resulting in a touchdown, and percentage of passes intercepted. This quarterback rating system is restricted to those quarterbacks who have a minimum of 1,500 passing attempts.

Takeaways/Giveaways

Takeaways and **giveaways** are two interesting pieces of football information that describe team turnovers. (Remember: turnovers refer to fumbles and interceptions.)

Takeaways refer to the number of times a team has taken the ball away from its opponents. Takeaways are calculated by adding the number of fumbles and the number of interceptions together. A team tries to have as many takeaways as possible throughout the season.

Giveaways, on the other hand, refer to the number of times a team gave up the ball to its opponents through fumbles and interceptions. As you can probably guess, a team tries to keep its number of giveaways as low as possible.

Let's look at a partial chart taken from the 1994-95 NFL Takeaway/Giveaway Information. We can see that Pittsburgh had 31 takeaways, having intercepted 17 passes and recovered 14 fumbles. We can also tell that the 1995 World Champions, the San Francisco 49ers, made 23 interceptions and recovered 12 fumbles for a total of 35 takeaways. If you look to the right to the giveaway side of the chart, you will notice that the Houston Oilers had more giveaways (42) than any other team in the NFL. They had 17 of their passes intercepted and lost 25 fumbles.

Team	Takeaways			Giveaways			Net Difference
	INT	Fum	Total	INT	Fum	Total	
Pittsburgh	17	14	31	9	8	17	+14
Kansas City	12	26	38	14	12	26	+12
San Francisco	23	12	35	11	13	24	+11
Green Bay	14	8	22	21	12	33	+11
Houston	14	12	26	17	25	42	-16
Cincinnati	10	8	18	19	22	41	-23

12.5 TAKEAWAYS/GIVEAWAYS

The last column on the chart, **Net Difference**, also called **turnover ratio**, refers to the difference between the number of takeaways and the number of giveaways. You will notice both positive and negative numbers in this column. A positive net difference indicates that the team has taken the ball away more times than it has given it up. A negative difference, on the other hand, indicates that the team had more giveaways than takeaways; in other words, it gave up the ball to its opponent more often than it took the ball away. The Green Bay Packers had a net difference of +11, meaning that they took the ball away 11 times more than they gave the ball away. The Cincinnati Bengals, on the other hand, had 23 more giveaways than takeaways, meaning that they gave up the ball 23 more times than they took it away.

As you might have guessed, the higher the positive number, the better the team's record tends to be; the higher the negative number, the worse its record is. By looking carefully at the number of its takeaways and giveaways, you can get a good idea of a team's performance.

Now that you have become familiar with some basic football numbers, you should be able to interpret the following 1994-95 NFL team information:

- The San Francisco 49ers became the first team since the 1984 Dolphins to score more than 500 points in one season, with a total of 506 points.

- The Minnesota Vikings' defense held opponents to fewer rushing yards than any NFL defense in the past 30 years.

- The Chicago Bears were penalized fewer times (65) for fewer yards (503) than any other team.

- The Tampa Bay Buccaneers ranked last in the NFL in number of sacks (20).

- The Dallas Cowboys led the NFL in total defense for the second time in three years.

- The New York Giants ranked last in the League in offense in 1994.

- The San Diego Chargers' placekicker John Carney led the NFL with 135 points (33 PAT's and 34 FG's).

- The Los Angeles (now Oakland) Raiders were assessed 156 penalties in 1994, which was an NFL record.

- The Denver Broncos' defense ranked 28th in the NFL, both in total yards allowed (5,907) and passing yards allowed (4,155).

- The Pittsburgh Steelers' defense had a good year; they led the NFL with a club-record 55 sacks, with linebacker Kevin Greene accounting for 14 of them (the best record in the NFL!).

Source: **Team NFL: The Official Magazine of the National Football League**: *1995 Preview. Vol. 5, No. 1. Los Angeles: National Football League Properties, Inc.*

Although I have presented examples of only a few tables, I suggest you try to keep an eye out for all types of football statistics. If you would like to apply the statistical football information you have learned, refer to books like *The 1995 Information Please Sports Almanac,* or *The Official National Football League Record and Fact Book.* Both are packed with all kinds of stats. You'll get a good workout trying to interpret them. Once you know the terms, acronyms, common abbreviations, and interpretations of these statistics, you'll be able to apply the information in whatever source you find them. The main thing to keep in mind is that even without an accompanying narrative, you can learn a lot about the game of football by simply looking at its numbers.

✅ CHAPTER 12 CHECKLIST
THINGS TO REMEMBER

- NFL Standings - A record of teams' performances
- Playoffs - Series of games played after the regular NFL season has concluded

TERMS TO KNOW

box score	standings	turnover ratio
giveaways	Super Bowl	wild card
single elimination	takeaways	

 EXTRA POINTS: DID YOU KNOW?

- Statistical records for all kinds of categories have been compiled and maintained by the National Football League from the year of its formation, 1920, to the present. Here are a couple of all-time Individual NFL Records (as of August 1995):

> Most yards rushing in a career - 16,726 - Walter Payton (1975-1987 Chicago Bears)

> Most touchdowns scored in a career - 139 - Jerry Rice (1985-1994 San Francisco 49ers)

> Most receptions in a career - 934 - Art Monk (1980-1993 Washington Redskins, 1994 New York Jets)

> Most yards gained passing in a season - 5,084 - Dan Marino (1983-present Miami Dolphins)

- By being a member of the 1995 World Champion team, the San Francisco 49ers' Ken Norton, Jr. has won three straight Super Bowl rings. In 1993 and 1994, he won Super Bowl rings as a Dallas Cowboy.

CHAPTER 13
WHO'S WHO IN THE NFL:
SOME NAMES TO REMEMBER

"That quarterback has all the mobility of the Chrysler Building."
- Kathy Mooney (1990)

Now that I have explained the game's fundamentals and have tried to carefully guide you through the minefield of football terminology, the professional football puzzle is almost complete. The last remaining piece involves the NFL players themselves.

To get a real flavor for the game, I believe it's necessary for you to become somewhat familiar with some of the most noteworthy names in the NFL, both active and retired. I often hear my students ask, "Oh, I've heard of so and so, what team does he play for?" or "Who are the major players I should know about on such-and-such team?"

This chapter gives you a brief introduction to some of the most well-known players in the NFL. I have categorized them by position and have included the jersey numbers, names, and the team on which they are listed (as of August 1995).

ACTIVE

Noted Quarterbacks

Number	Player
13	Dan Marino (Miami Dolphins)
12	Jim Kelly (Buffalo Bills)
7	John Elway (Denver Broncos)
11	Drew Bledsoe (New England Patriots)
8	Troy Aikman (Dallas Cowboys)
8	Steve Young (San Francisco 49ers)
1	Warren Moon (Minnesota Vikings)
12	Randall Cunningham (Philadelphia Eagles)
13	Jeff Hostetler (Oakland Raiders)

Noted Running Backs

Number	Player
22	Emmitt Smith (Dallas Cowboys)
27	Rodney Hampton (New York Giants)
20	Barry Sanders (Detroit Lions)
34	Thurman Thomas (Buffalo Bills)
28	Marshall Faulk (Indianapolis Colts)
20	Natrone Means (San Diego Chargers)

Noted Receivers

Number	Player
83	Andre Reed (Buffalo Bills)
80	Jerry Rice (San Francisco 49ers)
88	Michael Irvin (Dallas Cowboys)
80	Cris Carter (Minnesota Vikings)
87	Ben Coates (TE) (New England Patriots)
80	Andre Rison (Cleveland Browns)
80	Irving Fryar (Miami Dolphins)
81	Tim Brown (Oakland Raiders)

Noted Offensive Linemen

Number	Player
65	Bart Oates (C) (San Francisco 49ers)
77	William Roaf (T) (New Orleans Saints)
79	Erik Williams (T) (Dallas Cowboys)
61	Nate Newton (G) (Dallas Cowboys)

Noted Defensive Linemen

Number	Player
92	Reggie White (DE) (Green Bay Packers)
78	Bruce Smith (DE) (Buffalo Bills)
95	Richard Dent (DE) (San Francisco 49ers)
96	Cortez Kennedy (DT) (Seattle Seahawks)
94	Charles Haley (DE) (Dallas Cowboys)

Noted Linebackers

Number	Player
95	Greg Lloyd (Pittsburgh Steelers)
54	Chris Spielman (Detroit Lions)
55	Junior Seau (San Diego Chargers)
59	Seth Joyner (Arizona Cardinals)
55	Derrick Thomas (Kansas City Chiefs)

Noted Defensive Backs

Number	Player
42	Ronnie Lott (S) (Kansas City Chiefs)
29	Eric Turner (S) (Cleveland Browns)
26	Rod Woodson (CB) (Pittsburgh Steelers)
21	Deion Sanders (CB) (Dallas Cowboys)

Noted Kickers

Number	Player
3	John Carney (K) (San Diego Chargers)
10	Pete Stoyanovich (K) (Miami Dolphins)

2	Steve Christie (K) (Buffalo Bills)
5	Sean Landeta (P) (St. Louis Rams)
3	Rohn Stark (P) (Pittsburgh Steelers)
1	Reggie Roby (P) (Tampa Bay Buccaneers)

Noted Punt/Kick Return Specialists

Number	Player
23	Mel Gray (Houston Oilers)
34	Herschel Walker (New York Giants)
30	Dave Meggett (New England Patriots)
33	Tyrone Hughes (New Orleans Saints)
81	Tim Brown (Oakland Raiders)

These are just some of the many premier players who don NFL uniforms every week; keep your eyes and ears out for them each Sunday, and more often than not, you'll find they dominate the weekly football news.

The following players no longer play the game, but made tremendous contributions during their days in uniform. Some of these players have already been inducted into the Professional Football Hall of Fame, while some of the others will undoubtedly achieve that goal in the not-too-distant future. I have indicated the team(s) for which the player played and the years during which he played.

RETIRED
* indicates Hall of Fame inductee

Quarterbacks

*Bart Starr, Green Bay Packers (1956-71); inducted 1977

*Fran Tarkenton, Minnesota Vikings (1961-66, 1972-78), NY Giants (1967-71); inducted 1986

*Roger Staubach, Dallas Cowboys (1969-79); inducted 1985

*Terry Bradshaw, Pittsburgh Steelers (1970-83); inducted 1989

Joe Montana, San Francisco 49ers (1979-92), Kansas City Chiefs (1993-94)

Phil Simms, New York Giants (1979-93)

Running Backs

*Jim Brown, Cleveland Browns (1957-65); inducted 1971

*Gale Sayers, Chicago Bears (1965-71); inducted 1977

*O.J. Simpson, Buffalo Bills (1969-77), San Francisco 49ers (1978-79); inducted 1985

*Walter Payton, Chicago Bears (1975-87); inducted 1993

*Franco Harris, Pittsburgh Steelers (1972-83), Seattle Seahawks (1984); inducted 1990

Receivers

*Charley Taylor (WR), Washington Redskins (1964-75, 1977); inducted 1984

*Paul Warfield (WR), Cleveland Browns (1964-69, 1976-77), WFL (1975), Miami Dolphins (1970-74); inducted 1983

Charlie Joiner (WR), Houston Oilers (1969-72), Cincinnati Bengals (1972-75), San Diego Chargers (1976-86)

*Kellen Winslow (TE), San Diego Chargers (1979-87); inducted 1995

Offensive Linemen

*Forrest Gregg (OT), Green Bay Packers (1956, 1958-70), Dallas Cowboys (1971); inducted 1977

*Gene Upshaw (G), Oakland Raiders (1967-81); inducted 1987

*Art Shell (OT), Oakland Raiders (1968-81), Los Angeles Raiders (1982); inducted 1989

*John Hannah (G), New England Patriots (1973-85); inducted 1991

Defensive Lineman

*Joe "Mean Joe" Greene (DT), Pittsburgh Steelers (1969-81); inducted 1987

*Buck Buchanan (DT), Kansas City Chiefs (1963-75); inducted 1990

Dave Butz (DE-DT), St. Louis Cardinals (1973-74), Washington Redskins (1975-88)

Randy White (DE-DT), Dallas Cowboys (1975-88)

Linebackers

*Dick Butkus, Chicago Bears (1965-73); inducted 1979

*Jack Lambert, Pittsburgh Steelers (1974-84); inducted 1990

Harry Carson, New York Giants (1976-88)

Lawrence "L.T." Taylor, New York Giants (1981-94)

Defensive Backs

*Herb Adderley, Green Bay Packers (1961-69), Dallas Cowboys (1970-72); inducted 1980

Carl "Spider" Lockhart, New York Giants (1965-75)

*Willie Brown, Denver Broncos (1963-66), Oakland Raiders (1967-78); inducted 1984

Donnie Shell, Pittsburgh Steelers (1974-87)

Kickers

*George Blanda (K), Chicago Bears (1949-58), Baltimore Colts (1950), Houston Oilers (1960-66), Oakland Raiders (1967-75); inducted 1981

*Yale Lary (P), Detroit Lions (1952-53, 1956-64); inducted 1979

*Jan Stenerud (K), Kansas City Chiefs (1967-79), Green Bay Packers (1980-83), Minnesota Vikings (1984-85); inducted 1991

Ray Guy (P), Oakland Raiders (1973-81, 1982-86)

Dave Jennings, New York Giants (1974-84), New York Jets (1985-87)

Kick/Punt Return Specialists

Timmy Brown, Green Bay Packers (1959), Philadelphia Eagles (1960-67), Baltimore Colts (1968)

Billy "White Shoes" Johnson, Houston Oilers (1974-80), CFL (1981), Atlanta Falcons (1982-87), Washington Redskins (1988)

Terry Metcalf, St. Louis Cardinals (1973-77), CFL (1978-80), Washington Redskins (1981)

Rick Upchurch, Denver Broncos (1975-83)

The rosters of both the active and retired players change, of course, from year to year as new rookies are drafted into the NFL and many seasoned veterans "hang up their cleats" forever. I hope, however, that these brief listings have been helpful in getting you acquainted with the "stars," both past and present, of the National Football League. Trust me, the game is more fun and makes more sense if you can recognize a couple of names, numbers and faces.

CHAPTER 13 CHECKLIST
THINGS TO REMEMBER

To get a real flavor for the game of professional football, it is important to familiarize yourself with the current stars of the National Football League. It enhances your knowledge and enjoyment of the game when you can identify the premier NFL personalities.

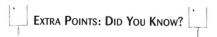

EXTRA POINTS: DID YOU KNOW?

- Ever wonder how NFL players keep themselves in shape during the off-season? According to Mark Kriegel of the New York Daily News, Herschel Walker, running back with the New York Giants, has a rather unorthodox daily regimen. His routine consists of a four mile run, a series of interval sprints, tae kwon do, another three or four mile run, and a series of astronomical repetitions of isometric exercises: between 750 and 1,500 push-ups, 500 dips and as many as 3,000 sit-ups! He does all this on one meal a day! Does this system work? In all his years of playing professional football, Walker has never gotten injured. He must be doing something right!

- Lawrence "L.T." Taylor was one of the most awesome linebackers in professional football. In his 13 seasons with the New York Giants, he racked up 132½ sacks, second only to Green Bay Packers defensive lineman Reggie White.

- Throughout the years, the sport of football has produced great nicknames for team units and players alike. Here's a small sample:

  "Purple People Eaters" – Defensive unit, Minnesota Vikings (1960's-1970's)

  "The Steel Curtain" – Defensive unit, Pittsburgh Steelers (1970's)

"Hogs" – Offensive linemen, Washington Redskins

"Secretary of Defense" – Deacon Jones, Defensive lineman, Los Angeles Rams (1960's)

William "The Refrigerator" Perry, Defensive lineman, Chicago Bears, Philadelphia Eagles (1980's-1990's)

"Sweetness" – Walter Payton, Running back, Chicago Bears (1970's - 1980's)

Deion "Prime Time" Sanders, Defensive back, Atlanta Falcons, San Francisco 49'ers and Dallas Cowboys (1990's). Sanders has also played professional baseball with the Atlanta Braves, Cincinnati Reds and now the San Francisco Giants.

Willie "Flipper" Anderson, Wide receiver, St. Louis (formerly Los Angeles) Rams (1980's-1990's)

"The Killer Bees" – Defensive unit, Miami Dolphins (1970's)

Ken "The Snake" Stabler, Quarterback, Oakland Raiders (late 1970's)

Ed "Too Tall" Jones, Defensive lineman, Dallas Cowboys (1980's)

"The Stick" – Candlestick Park, home field of the San Francisco 49ers

"Minister of Defense" – Reggie White, Defensive Lineman, Philadelphia Eagles and Green Bay Packers (1980's-1990's)

EPILOGUE

WATCHING PRO FOOTBALL: A WAY OF LIFE

*"At home on Sundays between 2 and 4 p.m.;
hope you are the same."* - Anonymous, 1969

There is a wooden plaque hanging in the den of my parents' home upon which the above words are written. It, of course, refers to the time when we all watched professional football games at our house. The plaque, which was a gift from my mother Jeanne to my father Frank, has been proudly displayed since 1969 on a wall along with all sorts of other family memorabilia. In its own way, it has symbolized a Mooney tradition that dates back as far as I can remember: professional football, and more specifically, the New York Giants.

I cannot actually recall the exact year I began to be interested in football; however, I do remember my father taking me to see a Giants game at Yankee Stadium in 1961. Since I was very young at the time, I don't remember too much of what happened that day, except for two things: 1) The Giants were playing the St. Louis Cardinals, and 2) I saw my first fake field goal. It was so great being in Yankee Stadium with all the fans and actually getting to see real live football players.

As I grew older I found myself sitting in front of the television every Sunday afternoon to watch my beloved Giants. In addition, to make the Giant games a little more interesting, my father and I had a wager every Sunday. In our household, my two sisters, Kathy and Mary Beth, and I had to do the dishes every night, Monday through Saturday. Since Sunday was our day off, my father would help my mother; that is, unless the Giants lost. My huge bet with my father: if the Giants won, he had to do the dishes and he paid me a quarter extra for my allowance. If the Giants lost, I had to do the Sunday dishes with no addition to my allowance. Since I have never wavered in my devotion to the Giants, and since they had quite a few years in which they struggled, there were many seasons I had dishpan hands from having to honor my part of the bet! I wonder if any of the Giants' players ever knew the extreme consequences I had to suffer because of their losing seasons?

No matter how busy our schedules have been through the years, my family would still find time to get together on Sunday afternoons in support of the Giants. My mother really never paid much attention to the games in the early years. (I can remember her wanting to go see the fall foliage on Sunday afternoons, but my father would good-naturedly tell her that if the Giants were playing, the only foliage she would be seeing would be from the 50-yard line!) However, she came to be quite a Giants fan during the later years of her life and actually looked forward to Sunday afternoons with the family and the Giants. Although my mother passed away in 1992, the family tradition continues to this day; we even use her tested recipes for the many Sunday dinners she graciously scheduled around Giants games throughout the years.

During my teenage years, I continued to watch the Giants faithfully and was lucky enough to go to a couple of games. At that time, my friends and I all had crushes on particular celebrities of the day; we would talk incessantly about this movie star or that rock and roll star. I shared their teenaged enthusiasm, but my "crush" was on who I thought to be one of the cutest guys ever to put on a New York Giants uniform: Tucker Frederickson. Frederickson (#24) was a running back from Auburn who was drafted by the Giants in 1965 and became one of the "Baby Bulls" in the Giants' backfield. All sorts of pictures of Tucker Frederickson adorned the inside of my locker during my high school years. None of my friends had any idea who this blond guy was, but that didn't matter at all to me. Tucker Frederickson was my idol.

It was also during this time that I met a man by the name of Tommy Di Nucci, one of the most loyal Giants fans I would ever know.

Tommy owned a little restaurant called the Pizza Oven in Fall River, Massachusetts, which my family and I frequented on our yearly camping trips to Cape Cod. Sometimes the Pizza Oven looked more like a shrine to the Giants than a restaurant; Tom, my father and I would pass the hours discussing our favorite topic: the Giants. Tommy was also the first person I ever knew to have had vanity license plates, his bearing the name JINTS.

How did Tommy get to be such a fanatic about the Giants? Years earlier, he had been in the U.S. Navy aboard the aircraft carrier USS Randolph with a man by the name of Wellington Mara, who is one of the principal owners of the Giants football team. One day when Mr. Mara and Tommy were on watch together, Mr. Mara asked him if he would like to see some home movies of his football team. Since Tom shared Mr. Mara's love of football, he agreed; and the rest, as they say, is history. After they got out of the Navy, Tom and Mr. Mara stayed in touch; Tom became a season's ticket holder and enjoyed many memorable times watching his Giants in person. It is through Tommy that I was able to see a few Giants games both at Yankee Stadium and at Giants Stadium (the Giants moved there in 1976) in East Rutherford, New Jersey.

Sad to say, Tommy Di Nucci passed away several years ago. At his funeral, Tommy was buried with some of his Giants memorabilia, and all his pall bearers wore New York Giants caps in his honor. When Tommy died, the "Jints" lost a loyal fan; Mr. Mara, my father and I lost a great friend; and the world lost a wonderful human being.

The Mooney tradition continued throughout the late 60's when I was fortunate enough to visit the summer training camps of both the New York Giants in Fairfield, Connecticut, and the Green Bay Packers at Lambeau Field in Green Bay, Wisconsin. Meeting Packer players Bart Starr, Paul Horning, and Jim Taylor; Giants players Homer Jones, Dick Lynch, and Don Chandler; and head coaches Allie Sherman (NY) and the legendary Vince Lombardi (GB) was quite an experience for me. I was even fortunate enough to get an autograph from Tucker Frederickson. Yes, *the* Tucker Frederickson!

Throughout the years I have followed the Giants through thick and thin, through the good years and those seasons when at times it seemed they couldn't even buy a victory. I cheered when they were 1987 and 1991 Super Bowl Champions, and moaned at their losses ("The Fumble" against the Philadelphia Eagles in 1978, and more recently on January 15, 1994, in a playoff game when they got destroyed by the San Francisco 49ers, 44-3).

In a strange sort of way these guys have been a part of my life for over 30 years and events in their lives have affected me. I can recall several years ago just how sad I felt when I learned that of one of my all-time favorite Giants, Carl "Spider" Lockhart, passed away from cancer; or when I watched Lawrence "L.T." Taylor being wheeled off the field in November 1992 after suffering what at the time was thought to be a career-ending Achilles tendon injury. Fortunately, L.T. came back to play his final season as a New York Giants linebacker in 1993-94 and then announced his retirement in January 1994. The list could go on and on. It's obvious that this team has had a profound impact on my life. Without their influence, I would neither be teaching a class on football fundamentals nor writing a book about football.

As I hope you can see, being a fan of professional football and a follower of the New York Giants for many years has added quite an enjoyable dimension to my life.

I honestly look forward to Sunday afternoons, and to teaching the football classes on Monday nights. Both activities are a great way to relax and have fun (yes, even when the Giants are in a close game!).

I welcome any comments you may have about this book. Please direct your correspondence to:

Dr. Patricia Mooney Gonzalez
Football Basics
P.O. Box 29
Newtonville, NY 12128

Good luck to each and every one of you. I sincerely hope that this book can help you in some way to create or enhance experiences similar to my own. Maybe it will help some of you to do battle with the dreaded "Green Ceiling" in the business world, to cope more constructively with your feelings of doom and gloom as each football weekend approaches, or better enable you to ward off football widowhood.

HOW MUCH DO YOU KNOW ALREADY?

(answers on p. xvi)

1. What is the NFL?_____

2. How many players can a football team have on the field at one time? _____

3. What is the offense?_____

4. Name the five ways a team can score points.
   a. _____
   b. _____
   c. _____
   d. _____
   e. _____

5. What are the dimensions of a football field?

   _____

6. How are inbound lines/hashmarks used? _____

   _____

7. What is the major responsibility of the referee?

   _____

8. Identify the jersey numbers assigned to running backs. _____

9. What is a down marker?_____

   _____

10. What is the shotgun formation? _____

_____

11. Name two of the player positions that make up
the offensive line.
a. _____
b. _____

12. What is the front four? _____

_____

13. What does a holder do? _____

_____

14. What is sudden death? _____

_____

15. What is decided during a coin toss? _____

_____

16. On what yard line do kickoffs originate? _____

17. Where are the "trenches" or the "pits"? _____

_____

18. How many minutes of playing time are there in a
regulation professional football game? _____

_____

19. What is the two-minute warning? _____

_____

20. How many time outs per half is each team allowed? _____

21. What is the down and distance rule?_____
_____

22. What happens during a bootleg play?_____
_____

23. What is the purpose of the pocket?_____
_____

24. What is a bomb? _____

25. What does the first digit in an alignment refer to?
_____

23. What is a dime defense? _____
_____

24. What is a blitz?_____
_____

25. Name two types of pass defense.
   a. _____
   b. _____

26. Name two of the six special team units on a football team.
   a. _____
   b. _____

27. How far does an onside kick have to travel to be legal? _____

28. What is hang time? _____

29. What is a fair catch? _____

30. On what yard line is the ball placed for an extra point attempt? _____

31. How many members make up an officiating crew?

_____

32. Who is the chief official? _____

33. How does an official signal that a touchdown, field goal, or extra point has been scored?

_____

37. What is a penalty marker? _____

_____

38. What are offsetting penalties? _____

_____

39. What does roughing the kicker mean? _____

_____

40. What is the amount of penalty yardage assessed for unsportsmanlike conduct? _____

APPENDIX A

FOOTBALL SCENARIOS: YOU BE THE COACH

(answers on p. 197)

1. Your team has a first down and ten. The quarterback hands off to his running back, who runs forward for a gain of seven yards. How do you describe the next play?

2. Your team has a second down and 5. Your quarterback is sacked behind the line of scrimmage for a loss of 7 yards. How do you describe the next play?

3. Your team has a first down on your opponent's 6-yard line and gains 2 yards. How do you describe the next play?

4. Your team has the ball on your opponent's 45-yard line and it is fourth down and 6. What would you do on the next play? Explain your choice.

5. Your team attempts a field goal. The ball is kicked, hits one of the uprights and falls behind the crossbar. Is the kick good? Why or why not?

6. Your opponent kicks off to your team, which has two kick returners waiting near your own end zone. One of the kick returners catches the ball in his own end zone and goes down on one knee. What does this signal? On what yard line will your offense start your next series of plays?

7. You are researching the opposing team for your next home game and want to know about its record so far. You check the NFL Standings and find the following information about your opponent: W-6, L-2, PF-125, PA-59, Home 6-0, Away 0-2, Div. 2-2. What can you tell about this team? In your own words, describe your opponent based on this standings information.

8. While doing more research in preparing for your next game, you find that your opponent has allowed very

little yardage to be gained against it "on the ground" (by running plays) and has inexperienced defensive backs. What type of game plans would you prepare for your team so that it matches up well against your opponent and you win the game?

9. A certain NFL team ends the season with a turnover ratio of -15. What conclusions might you draw about the team's overall performance based solely on this turnover ratio information?

10. Your opponent is in a fourth down situation on its own 25-yard line and is forced to turn the ball over to your team by punting. There are approximately three minutes to go in the game and you are trailing 24-21. During the punt, one of your linemen rushes in, tackles the punter without blocking the punt and receives a penalty for "roughing the kicker." What is your reaction to this chain of events? Why? Please be specific in your answer.

ANSWERS
FOOTBALL SCENARIOS: YOU BE THE COACH

1. Second down and 3 or second and 3.

2. Third down and 12 or third and 12.

3. Second down and goal from the 4 or second down and goal.

4. The best choice would be to punt the ball. Your team is not within field goal range (it would be a 62-yard field goal); if you punt the ball, your opponents would be forced to start their offensive series of plays deep in their own territory.

5. Yes, the kick is good. As long as the football falls behind the crossbar, it is a successful field goal.

6. It means that he is "downing the ball." He will not attempt to come on to the playing field, and will stay in his own end zone. The offense will begin the next series of plays on the 20-yard line.

7. This team has won six games and has lost two. It has won all of its home games, and lost both of its away ("on the road") games.

8. Since you know that this team has a good defense against running plays, you might not want to call too many running plays against them. You would probably try to pass as many times as possible, especially since this team's defensive backs do not have much experience in defending against a passing game.

9. A turnover ratio refers to the relationship between the number of times a team takes the ball away from its opponents and the number of times that they give the ball away to its opponents. A negative number indicates that this team gave the ball away more times than it took the ball away. In this case, they lost the ball 15 more times than they took it away.

10. When your opponent had a fourth down deep in its own territory, you know that it had to punt. That means you would have another opportunity to get the football and hopefully score. You have three minutes left in the game, and that is plenty of time for your team to move down the field. However, since you received a "roughing the kicker" penalty, your opponents receive an automatic first down and get to keep the football, instead of kicking it over to you. This chain of events is costly since your opponents now have the ball and have at least three more plays to gain enough yardage for a first down or to run out the clock to have the game end.

APPENDIX B
SUMMARY OF PENALTIES

Automatic First Down

All defensive fouls result in an automatic first down for the offense except in the following cases:

- Running into the kicker
- Excessive time out(s)
- Offside
- Delay of game
- Excessive celebrating by a player or players
- Illegal substitution
- Incidental grasp of facemask
- Encroachment

Loss of Down (No Yardage Assessed)

- A forward pass strikes the goal post, crossbar or the ground
- A forward pass goes out of bounds
- A forward pass touches or is caught by an ineligible receiver on or behind the line of scrimmage
- A forward pass is thrown from behind the line of scrimmage after the ball has already crossed the line
- A second forward pass is thrown behind the line of scrimmage
- A forward pass is first touched by an eligible receiver who has gone out of bounds and then returns in-bounds

Five yards

- False start
- First onside kickoff goes out of bounds between the goal lines and is not touched by either team

- Failure to pause one second after shift or huddle before starting a play
- Ineligible member or members of kicking team going beyond the line scrimmage before the ball is kicked
- Ineligible player or players downfield during a passing play
- Too many time outs
- Illegal motion
- More than 11 players on the field at the snap for either team
- Running into the kicker
- A 5-yard penalty or loss of team time out(s) on the defensive team for excessive crowd noise. It should be noted that the quarterback can be penalized if he does not make a satisfactory attempt to put the ball into play.
- Encroachment
- Illegal formation
- Illegal substitution
- Grasping face mask of opponent (incidental)
- Illegal return
- Delay of game
- Offside
- Failure of a member of either team to report change of eligibility
- Defensive holding or illegal use of hands (automatic first down)
- Illegal shift
- Invalid fair catch signal
- Less than seven players on the offensive line of scrimmage when ball is snapped
- More than one player in motion when the ball is snapped

- A player on either team is out of bounds when the ball is snapped
- Excessive or prolonged celebrations by an individual player or group of players

Ten Yards
- Helping the runner
- Offensive pass interference
- Tripping
- Deliberately kicking a loose ball
- Holding, illegal use of hands, arms or body by the offense
- Deliberately punching or batting a loose ball

Fifteen Yards
- Unsportsmanlike conduct
- Illegal blocking below the waist
- Any player uses the top of his helmet unnecessarily
- A player runs from beyond the line of scrimmage to attempt to block a point after touchdown or field goal and lands on other players
- Fair catch interference
- Roughing the kicker (automatic first down)
- Unnecessary roughness
- Delay of game at start of game or at start of second half
- A tackling player uses his helmet to spear, butt or ram an opponent
- A placekicker, holder or punter who fakes being roughed (tackled) by a defensive player
- Chop block
- Illegal crackback block by offense

- Roughing the passer (automatic first down)
- Twisting, pulling or turning an opponent by grasping his facemask
- Piling on (automatic first down)
- Clipping below the waist

Five Yards and Loss of Down
- Forward pass thrown from beyond (not behind) the line of scrimmage

Ten Yards and Loss of Down
- Intentional grounding of forward pass (this foul is called if the passer is in the pocket area between his two offensive tackles). If the passer intentionally grounds the ball in his own end zone, the defense is awarded a safety. If this foul occurs more than 10 yards behind the line of scrimmage, there is a loss of down at the spot of the foul.

Fifteen Yards and Loss of Coin Toss Option
- If either team arrives late on the field prior to scheduled kickoff
- If either of the team captains fail to appear for the coin toss

Fifteen Yards (and ejection/disqualification if the foul is flagrant)
- Unsportsmanlike conduct
- Roughing the kicker
- Hitting an opponent with a fist
- Unfair act – the referee determines the penalty yardage after consultation with other officials
- Malicious unnecessary roughness
- Kneeing or kicking an opponent

- Striking an opponent in his head or neck area with hands, elbow or forearm, whether or not the first contact is made below the neck area
- Roughing the passer

15 Yards and Automatic Disqualification

- A player uses his helmet as a weapon

Suspension from the Game

- A player or players may be suspended from the game for having illegal equipment. He may return to the game after one down when the referee decides that he is properly equipped.

APPENDIX C
FOOTBALL DO'S AND DON'TS: MISCELLANEOUS RULES

General

- There are five methods of scoring in professional football:
  a. Touchdown - 6 points
  b. Field Goal - 3 points
  c. Extra Point - 1 point
  d. Safety - 2 points
  e. Conversion - 2 points
- Kickoffs take place on the kicking team's 30-yard line.
- Each team is permitted to have 11 men on the field at the snap.
- If a kickoff goes above the crossbar and between the uprights of the opponent's goal post, it is not a field goal.
- The forward point of the ball is always used in measuring first down yardage.
- Any punt that touches the goal post is dead.
- If a player intercepts a pass in his own end zone and is downed, it is not a safety, but rather a touchback.
- Only team captains are allowed to talk to the officials.
- Player substitutions are unlimited. Players can enter the game only when the ball is dead. Players who leave the game must exit the playing area on their own team's side before the start of the next play.
- A quarter/period cannot end until play has been completed. If the defense commits a foul during the last play of the half or of the game, the offense may run another play.

- Players on the line must have both hands and both feet or a hand and both feet on the ground.
- No player is permitted to grab, twist, turn or pull an opponent's face mask.

Offense

- A running back or receiver carrying the ball may get up and continue to run if he slips and falls without actually being tackled or touched by an opposing player.
- The quarterback or other passer must be behind the line of scrimmage when he passes the football.
- A forward pass is ruled incomplete if any of the following occurs:
  a. The football is caught by the quarterback or passer.
  b. The football hits the goal post or the crossbar and is then caught.
  c. The football is caught out of bounds or hits the ground.
  d. The ball touches an ineligible receiver, then is caught by an offensive player.
  e. The player "traps" the ball; that is, he catches it at the same time it hits the ground.
- If a receiver goes out of bounds before a pass is thrown, he becomes ineligible.
- A forward pass is dead if it goes out of bounds, hits the goal post or touches the ground.
- A forward pass is ruled complete when the pass receiver catches the ball with both feet inbounds.
- Forward passes may be touched or caught by any eligible receiver. All defensive players are eligible receivers. On the offensive team, however, only the two ends on the line of scrimmage and the players in the backfield who are at least 1 yard behind the line of scrimmage are eligible receivers.

- A running back may ward off his opponents with his arms or hands (i.e., stiff arm technique) only when he is carrying the ball.

- No offensive player may assist a runner except by blocking for him.

- When offensive players legally block, they may make contact with the head, shoulders, hands, outer part of the forearm or any part of the body.

- A blocker is not permitted to use his arms or hands to push from behind, encircle or hang onto an opponent at any time.

- Offensive players may not link arms or hands to provide blocking for other team members. No interlocking interference is allowed.

- If two eligible receivers from opposing teams catch the ball at the same time, the football is awarded to the offensive team.

- When an offensive eligible receiver is hindered in his attempt to catch a forward pass by an opponent (in other words, interfered with) his team is awarded an automatic first down at the spot where the interference occurred.

- All players on the offensive team must be stationary when the football is snapped. There is one exception: one back may be in motion parallel to or behind the line of scrimmage.

- The offense must have at least seven players on the line of scrimmage. Those offensive players who are not on the line must line up at least one yard behind the line.

- Only the center's hands are allowed to be in the neutral zone. All other players must be on or behind their line of scrimmage.

- All members of the offense must "freeze" (come to a complete stop) without movement of feet, head or hands for at least one full second before the ball is snapped to begin play.

- If the offense is guilty of holding in its own end zone, the defense is awarded a safety worth 2 points.

Defense

- No defensive player is permitted to block an eligible receiver below the waist once the receiver goes beyond the line of scrimmage.

- Off the line of scrimmage, a defensive player is not permitted to make contact with an opponent above the shoulders with the palm of his hand toward him.

- A defensive player is not permitted to run into the quarterback (or other passer) after he has thrown a pass.

- No player may flagrantly hit a quarterback in the area of the knees or the head when approaching in any direction.

- A player is permitted to use his arms, hands and body when he is attempting to push or pull an opponent out of the way in a legal attempt to recover a loose ball.

- Defensive players have as much right to catch a pass as do offensive eligible receivers.

- A defensive player is not permitted to hinder an offensive receiver's attempt to catch a forward pass.

- A defensive player is permitted to make contact with an eligible receiver as long as he is looking for or making an attempt to catch or deflect a forward pass. He will not be penalized for defensive pass interference.

- Defensive players can line up anywhere behind their line of scrimmage.

- The defensive team can never score on a try-for-point (extra point). If the kick is blocked and the defense takes possession, the ball is dead.

- When a forward pass is clearly "uncatchable" (i.e., overthrown, underthrown, thrown off target to the receiver) and contact is made between the offensive eligible receiver and the defensive player, no defensive pass interference is called by the official.

Special Teams

- Intentionally running into the kicker/punter by members of the receiving team is not permitted.
- No kicking tees are permitted for points after touchdown (PAT) or field goal attempts. The kick must be made while the ball is in contact with the ground held on its end by a holder.
- The distance of a field goal is calculated by adding 17 yards to the distance between the point where the ball is placed and the defensive team's goal line. For example, if the ball were placed on the defense's 32-yard line, the kicking team would be attempting a 49-yard field goal.
- If a kickoff goes through the opponent's uprights, it is not a field goal.

Field

- The field must be 360 feet (120 yards) long and 160 feet (53 1/3 yards) wide.
- In the case of bad weather, it is the responsibility of the umpire to put down a new playable ball on every down.
- The sidelines and the end lines of a football field are out of bounds. The goal line is actually considered to be in the end zone. A player who has the ball scores when the ball is on, above, or over the goal line.

These are just a few of the many rules that apply to NFL games. For more detailed descriptions of all the NFL rules, please refer to the *NFL Digest of Rules* listed under **Recommended Reading** in Appendix D.

APPENDIX D
RECOMMENDED READING AND BIBLIOGRAPHY

Aversano, V. (ed.) *Football Digest: 1992 Annual Guide.* New York: Century Publishing Co., 1992.

Bragonier, R. *What's What in Sports: The Visual Glossary of the Sports World.* Maplewood, New Jersey: Hammond Incorporated, 1984.

Brock, T. and Campbell J. *The First Official NFL Trivia Book.* New York: New American Library, 1985.

Broido, B. *Spaulding Book of Rules and 1993 Sports Almanac.* Indianapolis, Indiana: Masters Press, Inc., 1992.

Foehr, D. P. *Football for Women and Men Who Want To Learn The Game.* Bethesda, Maryland: National Press Inc., 1988.

Foehr, D. P. *Touchdown: A Guide to Understanding and Enjoying Football.* Bloomfield Hills, Michigan: Franklin Press, 1993.

Horrigan, J. *The Official Pro Football Hall of Fame Answer Book.* New York: Simon and Schuster, Inc., 1990.

Korch, R. *The Official Pro Football Hall of Fame Playbook.* New York: Little Simon, 1990.

Madden, J. *One Knee Equals Two Feet And Everything Else You Need To Know About Football.* New York: Villard Books, 1986.

Meserole, M. (ed.) *The 1995 Information Please Sports Almanac.* Boston: Houghton Miffin Company, 1995.

National Football League 1995 Digest of Rules. New York: National Football League, 1995.

Neft, D. Cohen, R., and Korch, R. (eds.) *The Sports Encyclopedia: Pro Football.* New York: St. Martin's Press, 1992.

Nelson, C. *American Football*. London, England: Ward Lock Limited, 1991.

New York Giants Video Yearbook. Los Angeles, California: NFL Films.

The Official Book of Super Bowl XXIX: The Golden State of Football. San Francisco: Woodford Press, 1995.

Ominsky, D. and Harari, P.J. *Football Made Simple: A Spectator's Guide*. Los Angeles: First Base Sports, Inc., 1994.

Peterson's Sport Football: Pro Review. Los Angeles, California: Peterson Publishing Company.

Pincus, A. *How to Talk Football*. New York: Red Dembner Enterprises Corp., 1986.

Schiffer, D. and Duroska, B. (eds.) *Football Rules in Pictures*. New York: Putnam Publishing Group, 1992.

Seeman, J. (ed.) *1995 Official Playing Rules of the National Football League*. New York: The National Football League Properties, Inc., 1995.

Seeman, J. (ed.) *Make the Right Call: The Official Playing Rules of the NFL*. Chicago, Illinois, Triumph Books, 1993.

Team NFL 1995 Preview, Vol. 5, No.1. Los Angeles, CA: National Football League Properties.

The Official National Football League 1995 Record and Fact Book. New York: Workman Publishing Company, 1995.

Wilkinson, B. *Sports Illustrated Football: Defense*. New York: Harper and Row, 1984.

Wilkinson, B. *Sports Illustrated Football: Offense*. New York: Harper and Row, 1986.

APPENDIX E
NATIONAL FOOTBALL LEAGUE DIRECTORY

National Football League
410 Park Avenue
New York, NY 10022
(212) 758-1500

Arizona Cardinals
P.O. Box 888
Phoenix, AZ 85001
(602) 379-0101
Sun Devil Stadium
Capacity: 73,521
Grass

Atlanta Falcons
One Falcon Place
Suwanee, GA 30174
(404) 945-1111
Georgia Dome
Capacity: 71,280
Artificial turf

Buffalo Bills
One Bills Drive
Orchard Park, NY 14127
(716) 648-1800
Rich Stadium
Capacity: 80,290
Artificial turf

Carolina Panthers
227 W. Trade Street
Suite 1600
Charlotte, NC 28202
(704) 358-1644
Carolinas Stadium
Capacity: 72,500
Grass

Chicago Bears
Halas Hall
250 N. Washington
Lake Forest, IL 60045
(708) 295-6600
Soldier Field
Capacity: 66,950
Grass

Cincinnati Bengals
200 Riverfront Stadium
Cincinnati, OH 45202
(513) 621-3550
Riverfront Stadium
Capacity: 60,389
Artificial turf

Cleveland Browns
P.O. Box 679
80 First Avenue
Berea, OH 44017
(216) 891-5000
Cleveland Stadium
Capacity: 78,512
Grass

Dallas Cowboys
One Cowboys Parkway
Irving, TX 75063
(214) 556-9900
Texas Stadium
Capacity: 65,024
Artificial turf

Denver Broncos
13655 Broncos Parkway
Englewood, CO 80112
(303) 649-9000
Mile High Stadium
Capacity: 76,273
Grass

Detroit Lions
1200 Featherstone Road
Box 4200
Pontiac, MI 48342
(313) 335-4131
Pontiac Silverdome
Capacity: 80,836
Artificial turf

Green Bay Packers
1265 Lombardi Avenue
Green Bay, WI 54307
(414) 496-5700
Lambeau Field
Capacity: 59,543
Grass
Milwaukee County
Stadium
Capacity: 56,518
Grass

Houston Oilers
6910 Fannin Street
Houston, TX 77030
(713) 797-9111
Astrodome
Capacity: 62,439
Artifical turf

Indianapolis Colts
7001 West 56th Street
Indianapolis, IN 46254
(317) 297-2658
Hoosier Dome
Capacity: 60,129
Artificial turf

Jacksonville Jaguars
1 Stadium Place
Jacksonville, FL 32202
(904) 633-6000
Jacksonville Municipal
Stadium
Capacity: 73,000
Grass

Kansas City Chiefs
One Arrowhead Drive
Kansas City, MO 64129
(816) 924-9300
Arrowhead Stadium
Capacity: 78,067
Artificial turf

Miami Dolphins
Joe Robbie Stadium
2269 NW 199th Street
Miami, FL 33056
Joe Robbie Stadium
Capacity: 73,000
Grass

Minnesota Vikings
952 Viking Drive
Eden Prairie, MN 55344
(612) 828-6500
H.H. Humphrey Metrodome
Capacity: 63,000
Artificial turf

New England Patriots
Foxboro Stadium
Route 1
Foxboro, MA 02035
(508) 543-8200
Foxboro Stadium
Capacity: 61,000
Grass

New Orleans Saints
6928 Saints Drive
Metarie, LA 70003
(504) 733-0255
Louisiana Superdome
Capacity: 69,056
Artificial turf

New York Giants
Giants Stadium
East Rutherford, NJ 07073
(201) 935-8111
Giants Stadium
Capacity: 76,891
Artificial turf

New York Jets
1000 Fulton Avenue
Hempstead, NY 11550
(516) 538-6600
Giants Stadium
Capacity: 76,891
Artificial turf

Oakland Raiders
332 Center Street
El Segundo, CA 90245
(310) 322-3451
Oakland-Alameda County
Coliseum
Capacity: 50,000
Grass

Philadelphia Eagles
Veterans Stadium
3501 South Broad Street
Philadelphia, PA 19148
(215) 463-2500
Veterans Stadium
Capacity: 65,178
Artificial turf

Pittsburgh Steelers
Three Rivers Stadium
300 Stadium Circle
Pittsburgh, PA 15212
(414) 323-1200
Three Rivers Stadium
Capacity: 59,600
Artificial turf

St. Louis Rams
4245 N. Kingshighway
St. Louis, MO 63115
(314) 877-3700
The Domed Stadium at
America's Center
Capacity: 70,000
Artificial turf

San Diego Chargers
Jack Murphy Stadium
P.O. Box 609609
San Diego, CA 92160
(619) 280-2111
Jack Murphy Stadium
Capacity: 60,500
Grass

San Francisco 49ers

Marie P. DeBartolo
Sports Center
4949 Centennial Blvd.
Santa Clara, CA 95054
(408) 562-4949
Candlestick Park
Capacity: 61,513
Grass

Seattle Seahawks

11220 NE 53rd Street
Kirkland, WA 98003
(206) 827-9777
Kingdome
Capacity: 66,000
Artificial turf

Tampa Bay Buccaneers

One Buccaneer Place
Tampa, FL 33607
(813) 870-2700
Tampa Stadium
Capacity: 74,296
Grass

Washington Redskins

Redskin Park
P.O. Box 17247
Dulles Int'l Airport
Washington, DC 20041
(703) 478-8900
RFK Stadium
Capacity: 56,454
Grass

GLOSSARY OF FOOTBALL TERMS AND IDIOMS

ALIGNMENT The manner in which the defense lines up opposite the offense on the line of scrimmage before the ball is snapped and play begins.

ALL MADDEN TEAM A team of NFL players annually selected by sportscaster John Madden for their special contributions to the game of professional football.

ALL PRO Professional football players who are selected annually by football experts and coaches for their outstanding play.

ALL PURPOSE Category made by adding rushing, receiving and kick/punt return yardage together.

ALL THE WAY Reference to scoring a touchdown. If a player is going all the way, he is about to score a touchdown. Also called taking it to the house.

AMERICAN FOOTBALL CONFERENCE (AFC) One of two conferences which make up the National Football League, the other being the National Football Conference (NFC). Each conference is made of three divisions and 14 teams.

AT THE DOOR Refers to the situation when a team is near its opponent's goal line and is about to score.

ATTEMPTS (ATTS) The number of times a team tries to pass the ball, run with the ball, kick field goals or extra points, or make 2-point conversions.

AUDIBLE A signal called at the line of scrimmage by the quarterback to change the play he previously called in the huddle. Also called an *automatic*.

AUTOMATIC *See* audible.

BACK One member of a four-player unit (quarterback, right halfback, left halfback and fullback) who line up behind the offensive linemen.

BACK JUDGE (BJ) A member of the officiating crew who positions himself 17 yards deep on the same side of the field as the line judge. He keeps watch on the wide receiver and running back on his side of the field.

BACKFIELD (DEFENSIVE)   Collective unit made of the defensive backs (cornerbacks and safeties) who usually line up behind the linebackers. Their chief responsibility is to prevent the offense from completing passes. Also called the *secondary*.

BACKFIELD (OFFENSIVE)   The four players (quarterback, right halfback, left halfback and fullback) who line up behind the offensive linemen.

BACKUP   A player who serves as a substitute for another in the case of injury. If the starting quarterback cannot play, for example, the backup quarterback would take his place.

BAD SNAP   Refers to the action of the center as he delivers the ball to the quarterback, punter, or placekick holder. When there is a bad snap, the ball does not make it safely into the intended player's hands. Bad snaps can result in fumbles, lost yardage, blocked punts or blocked field goals.

BATTING   The intentional striking of the football with a hand or arm, such as when a defensive lineman bats down a quarterback's pass.

BEAT   Refers to when a player is able to get past an opponent who is trying to defend him (pass coverage), tackle him, or block him.

BLITZ   A defensive maneuver in which linebackers and/or safeties move across the line of scrimmage in an attempt to tackle the quarterback.

BLOCK/BLOCKER   A player uses any part of his body above his knees to obstruct an opponent by means of legal body contact.

BLOCKED KICK   A punt, field goal, or extra point attempt which is deflected by the defensive team.

BOMB   Another name for a long forward pass. You may hear the term used when a touchdown is scored: "He scored on a bomb."

BOOTLEG   A play in which the quarterback fakes a handoff to another player and carries the ball himself.

BOOTS IT THROUGH An expression meaning that a field goal or extra point was successful. If you hear of a kicker "booting it through," you know he made the field goal or extra point.

BOXMAN A member of the chain crew who handles the down marker/indicator, a 4-foot pole with four signs numbered 1, 2, 3 and 4 for the four downs. The boxman flips over the appropriate sign at the start of every play.

BREAK A TACKLE The ball carrier is hit by a defensive player but he is not tackled.

BREAK UP A PASS Action in which a defensive player knocks the football down before an offensive player, usually a receiver, is able to catch it.

BREAK UP A PLAY A maneuver in which a defensive player prevents an offensive play from being executed. For example, if a defensive back steps in front of a receiver awaiting a pass, and bats the ball away so the receiver can't catch it, he has broken up the play.

BRING DOWN To stop or tackle a ball carrier to the ground.

BRING IN THE CHAINS A signal given to the chain crew along the sideline to bring the down marker and 10-yard chain onto the field to measure the yardage needed for a first down.

BROKEN PLAY A play that isn't executed properly or doesn't go exactly as planned. Reasons for a broken play include a player's inability to remember the play that was called or a lineman blocking in the wrong spot. The quarterback, unfortunately, has to make the best of a bad situation and do some quick thinking on his feet to try to make the play successful. Sometimes broken plays result in horrendous consequences.

BULLET A forward pass thrown very hard. Some NFL quarterbacks are known for throwing bullets.

BUMP AND RUN A defense maneuver used by pass defenders in which they hit ("bump") a receiver once within 10 yards of the line of scrimmage. This is done to slow the receiver down; the defender must then run with the receiver and try to prevent him from catching a pass.

BYE An off date. It means that the team is not scheduled to play.

CADENCE At the beginning of each play, the quarterback calls a sequence of numbers and/or words to initiate the play. He had previously called this sequence in the huddles, and now uses the cadence as a signal for all of his teammates to move at the same time. Also called the *count*.

CALL A PLAY To tell players what specific play will be used. The quarterback usually calls the play, either himself or via the coaching staff.

CARRY The instance in which a player runs with the ball.

CENTER (C) Member of the offensive interior line who snaps the ball behind through his legs, usually to the quarterback who then directs the play. The center is able to make the snap quickly and then provide blocking. Also called the *snapper*.

CHAIN CREW/GANG A crew alongside the field responsible for the down marker and the 10-yard chain used to measure the distance needed for a first down, drive start, and forward stake indicator.

CHIP SHOT A term borrowed from golf. It refers to an easy field goal attempt, one which the placekicker is virtually assured of making.

CLIPPING A player runs, tackles, or dives into the back or the back of the legs of an opponent other than the player in possession of the football.

CLOTHESLINE TACKLE Tackling an opponent by thrusting an arm sideways into his Adam's apple. It is similar to running through a backyard and getting your neck caught by a clothesline.

COIN TOSS Takes place on the center of the field with the referee and the team captains within three minutes of the start of the game. The referee tosses the coin in the air and the captain of the visiting team calls "heads" or "tails." The winner of the coin toss chooses one of the following options: a) receive the ball; b) kickoff; or c) choice of goal his team will defend. The loser of the toss gets the alternative choice.

COMPLETION (COMP.)   A forward pass caught by an eligible receiver.

CONVERSION   A 1-point score made in a try-for-point attempt immediately after a touchdown. The team scoring the touchdown kicks the ball over the crossbar of its opponents' goal post.   A 2-point conversion can also be scored when the team just scoring the touchdown completes a pass in the opponents' end zone or runs the ball into the opponents' end zone.   Also called *Point After Touchdown (PAT)* or *extra point*.

CONVERSION   Refers to a team making a first down on either a third or fourth down play. A team "converts" a third or fourth down play into a first down.

CORNERBACK (CB)   Two members of the defensive backfield who line up closest to the sidelines and position themselves five to ten yards from the line of scrimmage. Their primary responsibility is pass defense.

COUGH UP THE BALL   Term referring to a player dropping or fumbling the ball.

COUNT   *See* cadence.

COUNTER PLAY   A running play in which the quarterback and offensive linemen are moving in one direction and the ball carrier is heading in the opposite direction.

COVERED   Synonymous with "defended." If a receiver is well defended or covered, it is wise for the quarterback to think twice about throwing a pass to him. If a receiver has double coverage, it means he is being defended by two players; it is not likely that a quarterback will throw a pass into "double coverage" unless he is feeling extremely lucky!

CROSSBAR   Part of a goal post consisting of a horizontal bar (18' 6" in length) placed 10 feet above the ground. Attached on each end is a vertical pole called an upright.

CUT   Refers to any quick change of direction on the part of a ball carrier.

CUTBACK Refers to a quick change in the direction of a run in response to the direction of the pursuit (tacklers). This maneuver is used primarily by receivers and ball carriers.

DEAD BALL The football becomes "dead" when the play is over; when the ball is snapped to begin the next play, it becomes "live" again. When the ball is dead, it may only be touched by an official.

DEAD BALL FOUL A foul that occurs when the play is over and the ball is dead.

DEEP MAN Term used to describe a defensive back, punt returner, or pass receiver who is far away (downfield) from the action occurring at the line of scrimmage.

DEFENSE The team that defends its goal. It does not have possession of the ball and tries to prevent the offense from advancing the ball and scoring.

DEFENSIVE ALIGNMENT *See* alignment.

DEFENSIVE HOLDING Illegal use of the hands when attempting to block an offensive player.

DEFENSIVE LINE Defensive unit consisting of two defensive tackles (DT) and two defensive ends (DE). Sometimes called the "front four." The defensive line is usually made up of the largest defensive players.

DEFENSIVE PASS INTERFERENCE Illegal interference with an offensive player's opportunity to catch a forward pass.

DEFENSIVE TACKLE One of two defensive linemen who lines up between the ends when there are four linemen on the front line.

DELAY OF GAME Any failure by a team to be ready for play within the specified time limit or any action that delays the game.

DOUBLE COVERAGE Two players on one team assigned to block or run pass coverage against one man on the other team. Also called *double teaming*.

DOUBLE FOUL Infraction of the rules by both teams on the same play.

DOUBLE TEAMING *See* double coverage.

DOWN The basic unit of play in football. Each play in a football game is a down. The team with the ball (offense) has four downs in which to advance the ball 10 yards.

DOWN MARKER A four-foot pole with four signs numbered 1, 2, 3, and 4, which are flipped over at the start of every play. The down marker marks the forwardmost point of the ball at the start of every play and displays the number of the down.

DOWN THE BALL Action of the kick returner who catches the ball and who goes down on one knee to stop the play. A player often "downs" the ball on a kickoff when he catches the ball in the end zone and does not wish to step onto the playing field.

DOWNFIELD The area beyond the line of scrimmage in the scoring direction of the offense.

DRAW PLAY A running play in which the quarterback initially drops back as if to pass, then hands the ball off to a running back.

DRAWN OFF Any movement or act of the offense designed to cause the defense to move across the line of scrimmage before the ball is snapped. Sometimes the movement of the quarterback's head as he calls the play on the line of scrimmage "draws off" the defense.

DRIVE The series of plays that an offensive team uses as it moves up and down the field. If the drive results in a score, it is called a *scoring drive*. The measurement of the drive begins when the offense first takes possession of the ball and ends when it either scores, punts, or turns the ball over to the defense by fumble or interception.

DROP BACK The action in which the quarterback, after receiving the ball from the center, moves away from the line of scrimmage before making a forward pass. Also called fade back.

DUMP OFF The action in which the quarterback throws a pass to a receiver who is nearby but who was not his primary target. Generally, you will see a quarterback dumping the ball off when all of his receivers are well-defended, or in response to pressure put on him by the defense.

ELIGIBLE RECEIVER Any defensive player or any of five offensive players (two ends on the scrimmage line and three players in the backfield other than the passer) who are allowed to catch a forward pass.

ENCROACHMENT When a player, usually a lineman, moves into the neutral zone and makes contact with an opposing player before the ball is snapped.

ENDLINES The lines at the end of the field 10 yards beyond the goal lines.

END-OVER-END Refers to the movement of a kicked ball when it is spinning from one point of the ball to the other.

END ZONE An area 10 yards deep located at each end of the field. Touchdowns and safeties are scored here.

EXHIBITION GAME A game whose outcome has no effect on team or league standings or player/team records. In the National Football League, the regular exhibition season begins in August of each year. Also called *pre-season.*

EXTRA POINT A single point earned by a team for a successful placekick immediately after it has scored a touchdown. Also known as *Point After Touchdown (PAT)* or *conversion.*

FACE MASK A plastic structure resembling a bird cage that is attached to the player's helmet to protect the face.

FADE BACK *See* drop back.

FAIR CATCH Signal used by receiver of a kick (either kickoff or punt) to indicate that he will not try to advance the ball once he catches it. The player signals a fair catch by raising one arm full length above his head and waving it from side to side while kick is in flight. Once he signals a fair catch, he is protected against being tackled.

FAIR CATCH INTERFERENCE A member of the kicking team interferes with the fair catcher, the ball, or his path to the ball.

FALSE START A player charges or moves after assuming a set position before the ball is snapped and the play is over.

FIELD GOAL (FG) A team scores a field goal worth 3 points when the kicker place-kicks the football from the line of scrimmage over the opposing team's crossbar.

FIELD POSITION Refers to the location of the football on the field. When the offense has the ball near the opposing team's goal line, it has good field position. On the other hand, when the offense has the ball deep in its own territory, near its own goal line, it has poor field position.

FIRST DOWN When the team in possession of the ball has a first down, it has four plays (downs) in which to gain 10 yards for another first down. When the offensive team makes a first down, the referee points towards the defensive team's goal.

FIRST STRING Refers to the starting lineup of a football team. Usually the best players are members of the first string. Those players who substitute for the first string players are the second string.

FLAG A yellow handkerchief-sized flag carried by the official and thrown to the ground when a foul occurs. Also called penalty flag or penalty marker.

FLAG ON THE PLAY A member of the officiating crew throws a yellow flag/penalty marker to indicate that a foul has been committed. He throws the flag near the spot of the infraction.

FLANKER (FL) The wide receiver on the tight end's side of the field who lines up at least one yard behind the line of scrimmage.

FLEA FLICKER An offensive play designed to trick the defense into thinking a running play will occur. During a flea flicker, the quarterback hands the football off to a running back who pitches the ball back to the quarterback who then passes.

FORMATION The way the offensive and defensive teams position themselves (line up) at the beginning of each play.

FORWARD PASS A football that is thrown in the direction of the opponent's goal line by the quarterback or another offensive player. Only the offensive team may throw a forward pass. The pass must be thrown in or behind the neutral zone.

FORWARD PROGRESS The spot on the field to which the ball carrier has advanced the ball, even if his opponents had pushed him backwards after getting there.

FORWARD STAKE INDICATOR A large, vinyl, brightly colored arrow placed on the ground on the sideline to indicate the spot to which a team must advance to get a new first down.

FOUL Any violation of a rule. An official throws the yellow flag to the ground to indicate a foul has been committed. The referee signals the infraction of the rule and assesses the penalty against the team guilty of the violation.

FREE BALL Refers to a live ball in play, except for a forward pass that is not in possession of any player.

FREE SAFETY One of the members of the defensive backfield between the cornerbacks. The free safety usually positions himself on the opposite side of the ball from the tight end. Also called *weak safety*.

FRONT FOUR The forward defensive line consisting of two tackles and two ends.

FULLBACK (FB) One of two types of running backs (RB), the other being the halfback (HB). Generally, a fullback is bigger, usually carries the ball up the middle for short yardage, and provides blocking on other offensive plays.

FUMBLE When a player loses possession of the ball (that is, drops or otherwise mishandles). The term "coughing up the ball" is also used to refer to fumbling.

GAME PLAN A plan consisting of game strategies and all the plays and techniques necessary to carry it out successfully. Specific game plans are determined by the coaching staff who has spent considerable time evaluating opposing teams.

GO AGAINST THE GRAIN Movement opposite from the direction that most players are going. If the quarterback, offensive linemen, and receivers are moving to the left, for example, and the ball carrier moves to his right, that ball carrier is going against the grain.

GOAL LINE The line that has to be crossed by the team in possession of the ball in order to score a touchdown. There are two goal lines, both parallel to the end lines one at either end of the field and separate the end zones from the 100-yard field of play.

GOAL POST Set behind each end line. Consists of a horizontal crossbar and a pair of vertical uprights. There are two goal posts on each football field.

GO FOR IT Refers to the fourth down situation in which the offense tries to gain enough yardage for a new first down, rather than punt to its opponent or attempt a field goal.

GOOD HANDS Attribute possessed by those players such as running backs, wide receivers, defensive backs, and kick returners, who can handle the football well.

GRASPING OPPONENT'S FACE MASK When a player grabs, twists, turns, or pulls an opponent by the face mask. This is not permitted and players get penalized for this infraction.

GRIDIRON A slang term for the playing field. The pattern of lines on the field resembles the cooking utensil used to broil foods.

GRIND IT OUT A strategy in which a team gains yardage in small amounts by using running plays or short passes.

HAIL MARY A long forward pass in which the quarterback just throws it up and "prays" that one of his receivers will catch it. The Hail Mary pass is usually thrown into the opponent's end zone in a last ditch effort to score a touchdown.

HALF A football game is divided into two halves; each half is divided into two periods or quarters of 15 minutes each.

HALFBACK (HB) One of two types of running backs (RB), the other being the fullback (FB). Generally, a halfback is the smallest and speediest of the running backs.

HALFTIME The 12-minute intermission between the two halves of a football game.

HANDOFF The exchange of the football from one offensive player to another, such as when the quarterback hands off to a running back.

HANG TIME The number of seconds between the time the punter kicks the ball and the time the punt returner catches it.

A punter wants to have his "hang time" be as long as possible so that his teammates have enough time to get downfield to tackle the kick returner who has caught the ball and is trying to advance it.

HASHMARKS Lines parallel to the sidelines that extend from one goal line to the other and measure 70' 9" from the sidelines.

HAVE/GET YOUR BELL RUNG When a player has his bell rung, he gets hit so hard he feels vibrations as if his head were inside a gonging bell. You may also hear some announcers refer to this as a player getting "dinged."

HEAD LINESMAN (HL) A member of the officiating crew who positions himself on the line of scrimmage. His responsibilities include supervision of the chain gang and looking for infractions on the line of scrimmage.

HEAR FOOTSTEPS A player who hears footsteps becomes aware that he is about to be hit by a defensive player. Often when a player hears footsteps, he loses concentration on his assigned task and may be unable to execute it properly.

HIT Quarterback term. When a quarterback "hits" a receiver, he completes a pass to him.

HOLDER Player who holds the football upright on the ground for the kicker during conversions and field goal attempts.

HOLE A gap or space created for a ball carrier by his blockers.

HOT DOG A player who tries to show up his opponent by excessive gesturing and movements. You may see players do little dances, cartwheels, flips, point fingers, and use other well-known hot dog maneuvers to celebrate a success such as scoring a touchdown or sacking a quarterback.

HUDDLE Before each play, players get together in a group on the field, usually forming a circle. In the huddle, the players decide on the strategy and the signals for the next play. Both offensive and defensive teams may huddle to determine what plan to follow.

ILLEGAL MOTION A player or players are illegally in motion before the ball is snapped.

ILLEGAL PROCEDURE Movement of a member of the offensive line after the team is set, but before the ball is snapped.

ILLEGALLY PASSING OR HANDING THE BALL FORWARD When the passer throws or hands the ball off from beyond (not behind) the line of scrimmage.

INBOUND LINES Lines parallel to sidelines. Extend from one goal line to the other and measure 70' 9" from the sidelines. Also called hashmarks.

INCOMPLETION A forward pass that is dropped, hits the ground, caught out of bounds, not intercepted, or is otherwise not completed. Also known as *incomplete forward pass*.

INELIGIBLE RECEIVER An offensive player, usually a center, guard, or tackle, who is not permitted to catch a forward pass.

INELIGIBLE RECEIVER DOWNFIELD An offensive player who is not designated as an eligible receiver (e.g., a lineman) should not be downfield.

INJURED RESERVE (I.R.) This is an official list of players who are recuperating from injuries and, as a result, are not listed on a team roster.

INTENTIONAL GROUNDING The quarterback deliberately throws an incomplete pass in order to avoid being tackled behind the line of scrimmage.

INTERCEPTION (INT.) A pass intended for an offensive player that is caught by any defensive player before it hits the ground. Once the player has possession of the ball, he may run with it.

INTERFERENCE The offensive player(s) who block in front of the ball carrier.

INTERIOR LINE/LINEMEN Group of offensive players in the middle of the line who work together as a unit. The interior line consists of a center (C), two guards (G), and two tackles (T). They block for the ball carriers, passers, and pass receivers.

INVALID FAIR CATCH SIGNAL Failure of the kick receiver to give a proper fair catch signal.

KICKOFF The method of starting play at the beginning of the game, at the start of the second half, or after a field goal or extra point has been scored. Kickoffs originate on the kicking team's 30-yard line.

LATERAL A lateral is a pass that travels backward or parallel to the goal line. Any player may lateral the football to a teammate at any time. Also known as a *backward pass*.

LINEBACKER (LB) A defensive player who lines up in an upright position just behind the defensive line. Most defenses line up with either three or four linebackers.

LINE JUDGE (LJ) A member of the officiating crew who stands on the line of scrimmage opposite the head linesman.

LINEMAN One of the seven offensive players positioned on the line of scrimmage: the center, two guards, two tackles and two ends.

LINE OF SCRIMMAGE Imaginary lines from the tip of the football that run parallel to the goal line and straight across the field. The two opposing teams line up on these two lines.

LONG SNAPPER The special center who snaps the ball back to the punter or placekicker during kicking situations.

MAN-FOR-MAN A defensive formation in which each player is assigned to cover or guard a specific player on passing plays.

MAN-IN-MOTION One member of the offensive backfield may be moving before the ball is snapped. When the ball is snapped, he must be moving away from or parallel to the defensive team's goal line.

MAN-TO-MAN *See* man-for-man.

MIDFIELD The 50-yard line that divides the playing field into two parts.

MOMENTUM Refers to the situation in which everything is going right with a particular team. If you hear announcers say things like "Momentum is with the 49ers this half" or "Mo' is hanging out with San Francisco," you'll know that the San Francisco 49ers are in the position of having everything go their way.

MONDAY MORNING QUARTERBACK A person who thinks he or she is an expert at indicating what a team could have done or should have done during a game that has already been played. Since most NFL teams play on Sunday afternoons, this second guesser does his or her best work on Monday mornings.

MOVE THE CHAINS/STICKS When a team gains enough yardage for a first down, a new 10-yard distance needs to be marked off and the yardage chains/sticks have to be moved.

MUFF The touching of a loose ball by a player in an unsuccessful attempt to gain possession.

MULTIPLE FOUL Two or more fouls are committed by the same team on the same play.

NATIONAL FOOTBALL CONFERENCE (NFC) One of the two conferences that make up the National Football League, the other being the American Football Conference (AFC). Each conference is made up of 3 divisions and contains 15 teams.

NATIONAL FOOTBALL LEAGUE (NFL) National Football League, composed of 30 teams organized into two conferences, the National Football Conference (NFC) and the American Football Conference (AFC).

NEUTRAL SITE A site for a football game which is not the home field of either team. The Super Bowl is usually played at a neutral site; for example, Super Bowl XXIX between the San Francisco 49ers and the San Diego Chargers was held at Joe Robbie Stadium in Miami, Florida.

NEUTRAL ZONE An area the length of the football located between the offensive and defensive lines of scrimmage.

NICKEL BACK The fifth defensive back in an alignment.

NICKEL DEFENSE A defensive alignment that has five defensive backs instead of the usual four.

NO HUDDLE OFFENSE Series of plays that the offense uses without conferring first in the huddle. The team just lines up and starts the play. No-huddle offenses are used when the team needs to move the ball quickly (e.g., at the end of the first half

NOSETACKLE   A defensive lineman who lines up directly opposite the offensive team's center. Also called *nose guard* or *middle guard.*

OFF TACKLE   A running play in which the ball carrier runs into the line outside of his offensive tackle, rather than running directly ahead.

OFFENSE   The team in possession of the football.

OFFENSIVE HOLDING   Illegal use of the hands while blocking a defensive player.

OFFENSIVE LINE/LINEMAN   The offensive line consists of a center, two guards, and two tackles. Since there must be seven offensive players on the line of scrimmage when the ball is snapped, the term "offensive line" may also include the two ends.

OFFENSIVE PASS INTERFERENCE   The receiver hinders the progress of a defensive player who is trying to catch the ball on a passing play.

OFFICIAL   One of a seven-member crew in charge of running the game. The referee, who wears a wireless microphone and a white cap, is the captain of this crew.

OFF-SETTING PENALTIES   Occurs when both teams are guilty of rule infractions on the same play. The penalties assessed by the officials cancel each other out.

OFFSIDE   A player is offside when any part of his body crosses the line of scrimmage before the ball is snapped.

ONSIDE KICK   A short kickoff, which must travel a minimum of 10 yards, used by the kicking team in hopes that the receiving team will mishandle the ball and the kicking team will take possession.

OPTION   Offensive play in which the quarterback runs along the line of scrimmage with the choice of keeping the ball, throwing it or handing it to a running back.

OUT OF BOUNDS   The area encompassing the sidelines, the endlines, and the areas beyond them. A player or football touching the sideline or endline is considered to be out of bounds. When any part of the ball or the ball carrier touches the out of bounds marker, the play is over and the ball is dead.

OVERTIME (OT) When the score is tied at the end of regulation time in a football game, both teams continue to play in a 15-minute block of time called the overtime period. *See* sudden death.

OWN GOAL The goal a team is defending.

OWN TERRITORY The area between a team's own goal line and the 50-yard line (midfield).

PASS PATTERN A series of movements or maneuvers run by a receiver on a pass play.

PASS RUSH The attempt by the defensive team to penetrate past the offensive linemen to tackle the quarterback before he can throw the football.

PASSER Player who throws the football.

PASSING PLAY A play that involves throwing or passing the football as opposed to running.

PASSING TREE A passing diagram that, when drawn on a blackboard, looks very much like a leafless tree. The branches on the tree represent the various pass routes a receiver can run. There are passing trees for wide receivers, tight ends and running backs.

PATTERN *See* pass pattern.

PENALTY Punishment given by the officiating crew when players commit a foul or violate the rules during a game. Penalties can include the loss of a down, the loss of yardage, player ejection, or sometimes all three, depending upon the severity of the infraction.

PENALTY FLAG *See* flag.

PENALTY MARKER *See* flag.

PERIOD One of four 15-minute components of a football game. Also called a *quarter*.

PERSONAL FOUL An illegal tactic that can cause injury. The team that commits a personal foul is assessed a penalty.

PICK Slang term for interception. A defensive back wants to have as many "picks" during the season as he can.

PICK OFF Synonymous with intercept. When a defender picks off a pass, he intercepts it; that is, he catches the ball that was intended for an offensive player before it hits the ground. Interceptions are sometimes referred to as "picks."

PICK UP Gain in yardage. If a ball carrier picks up 5 yards or makes a pick up of 5 yards, it means he has gained 5 yards.

PIGSKIN Slang term used to describe a football, although footballs are actually made out of cowhide.

PILING ON A defensive player or players deliberately falls or throws himself upon a downed ball carrier after the referee's whistle has sounded signaling the play has ended.

PITCH/PITCHOUT A short underhand lateral toss of the football, generally from the quarterback to a running back.

PITS Refers to the place where the interior line (made up of the left tackle, left guard, center, right guard, and right tackle) meets the defensive linemen. Also called the *trenches*.

PLATOON A unit of a football team, usually consisting of two or more sections. Professional football uses a two-platoon system (offense and defense), which allows for the substitution of players.

PLAY-ACTION PASS A play in which the quarterback fakes a hand-off to a running back before he passes the ball.

PLAY CLOCK The clock that displays the number of seconds that the offense has to start a play. Also called the *second clock* or the *40/25 second clock*.

POCKET A protective wall usually formed by the offensive linemen and running backs behind which the quarterback retreats as he prepares to pass.

POINT AFTER TOUCHDOWN (PAT) A one (1) point score made immediately following a touchdown. Also called a *conversion* or *extra point*.

POSSESSION Refers to any player who holds or controls the ball long enough legally to perform acts in a football game.

PREVENT DEFENSE A defensive formation that includes extra defensive backs to provide additional pass coverage against an expected long pass. A prevent defense allows short gains to be made, but it guards against long gains and scoring by the offense.

PRIMARY RECEIVER The receiver to whom the quarterback plans to throw a pass.

PUNT The player designated as the punter "punts" the ball by first dropping it, then kicking it before it hits the ground.

PUNT RETURN The act of catching and advancing a punt by a punt returner.

PUNT RETURNER The special team's player whose specialty is returning punts.

PUNTER A member of one of the special teams whose expertise is punting.

PYLON Flag on a flexible pole located at each corner of the end zone.

QUARTER *See* period.

QUARTERBACK (QB) Leader of the offensive team. Also called the passer or "field general." He lines up directly behind the center, so he can be handed the ball directly through the center's legs to direct the play.

READ THE BLITZ Refers to the offense's reaction to the defensive alignment. If the quarterback "reads blitz," he suspects that members of the defense (linebackers and/or safeties) are going to rush in to sack him.

READ THE DEFENSE The quarterback recognizes what alignment the defense has set up to counter his play. He may then call an audible; that is, change the play at the line of scrimmage.

RECEIVER (R) The player to whom a football is passed.

RECOVER To gain (or regain) possession of a fumbled football.

RED ZONE The area between the opponent's goal line and its 20-yard line.

REFEREE (R) The official in charge of the officiating crew. He is the only crew member to wear a white cap and a wireless microphone. He positions himself 10 to 15 yards behind and off to the side of the quarterback.

RETURN A runback of an intercepted pass, punt, or a kick.

REVERSE An offensive play designed to confuse the defense. The quarterback hands the ball off to a running back, who runs towards the sideline; the running back, in turn, hands the ball off to a runner who is going in the opposite direction.

ROLLOUT Passing play in which the quarterback/passer retreats a short distance behind the line of scrimmage and then runs toward the sideline before throwing. This maneuver helps the quarterback avoid tacklers and gives him more time to find a receiver.

ROOKIE A player who is playing in his first year of professional football.

ROSTER A list showing names, positions, and other information about the players on a football team.

ROUGHING THE KICKER A member of the kick receiving team tackles or runs into the kicker or punter in a violent manner. The team guilty of the violation is assessed a penalty that varies, depending upon whether the guilty player or players ran into or "tackled" the kicker.

ROUGHING THE PASSER Running into or tackling the quarterback after the football has left his hand. As in a "roughing the kicker" situation, a penalty is assessed for "roughing the passer." Also called *roughing the quarterback*.

ROUGHING THE QUARTERBACK *See* roughing the passer.

RUNNING BACK (RB) An offensive player who lines up at least one yard behind the line of scrimmage and who runs with the ball. The term includes halfback and fullback.

RUSHER Player who rushes (runs) with the ball.

RUSHING Running with the ball on a play from the line of scrimmage. Rushing information deals with the running performance of individuals and/or teams.

SACK To tackle the quarterback behind the line of scrimmage for a loss of yardage while he is attempting to pass. If two defensive players tackle the quarterback at the same time, each is awarded a half sack.

SAFETY (1) A 2-point score made by the defense. Only the defense can score a safety. The ways a team can earn a safety include: 1) if it tackles a ball carrier in his own end zone; 2) if the ball carrier steps out of the back or side of his own end zone; and 3) if a blocked punt goes out of the end zone, or 4) if the offense is guilty of holding in its own end zone.

SAFETY (2) One of the members of the defensive backfield. There are two safeties, a strong safety and a weak safety, and two cornerbacks, whose major responsibility is to provide pass coverage.

SAFETY BLITZ Occurs when one or two safeties suddenly rush towards the quarterback instead of dropping back to play pass defense.

SAFETY VALVE The player to whom a quarterback often throws when he is under a lot of pressure from the defense and needs to get rid of the ball in a hurry. A quarterback throws the ball to a safety valve who is not his primary receiver but may be positioned near the line of scrimmage.

SCORE A touchdown (6 points), field goal (3 points), or conversion (1 point or 2 points) has been made. The referee extends both arms above his head. If a safety (2 points) has been scored, the referee places his palms together over his head.

SCOREBOARD A large board in the stadium that displays the score of the game and other pertinent information such as down, yards to go for a first down, quarter, time outs, time remaining in the quarter or the game, and the team with the ball.

SCORING DRIVE A drive which results in a score. *See* drive.

SCRAMBLE Refers to the action of the quarterback trying to evade defenders while looking for a pass receiver downfield.

SCREEN PASS An offensive play in which the defensive linemen are allowed to get through the offensive line. The quarterback then drops a short pass over the linemen's heads to a receiver who is still behind the line of scrimmage.

SCRIMMAGE The action that results when a play starts. A scrimmage begins when the center snaps the ball back and ends when the ball is whistled dead by the officials.

SECOND CLOCK *See* play clock.

SECOND STRING The unit of a football team which serves as substitutes for any of the members of the starting lineup or first string. If any of the starters get injured or have to be out of the game for any reason, members of the second string team take their place.

SECONDARY Unit of the defensive team consisting of two safeties and two cornerbacks. Secondary also refers to the area of the field covered by these men. Also called *defensive backfield*.

SECONDARY RECEIVER The receiver to whom the quarterback looks to pass if his primary receiver is well-defended.

SET *See* formation.

SHANK To punt the ball of the side of the foot. When a punter "shanks it," he usually sees his punt travel erratically for only a very short distance.

SHED A TACKLER To break away from a tackler who has already grabbed a ball carrier. A good running back often has a reputation of shedding tacklers, meaning that he is able to break away and continue running although tacklers have already had their hands on him.

SHIFT The movement of two or more offensive players who change position after lining up but before the ball is snapped.

SHOTGUN FORMATION Offensive formation in which the quarterback lines up at least 5 yards behind the center instead of directly behind him.

SHOWING BLITZ Describes the alignment in which the defensive players (the linebackers and/or the defensive backs) indicate that they may blitz (rush in to tackle the quarterback) once the play begins.

SIDE JUDGE (SJ) A member of the officiating crew who lines up 17 yards deep on the same side of the field as the head linesman. He keeps watch on the wide receiver and running back on his side of the field.

SIDELINE The lines at the sides of the field running the entire length of the field. The sidelines separate the out-of-bound areas from the playing area of the field.

SINGLE ELIMINATION The system in football in which a team is eliminated from further competition after only one loss. The NFL playoffs are based on the single elimination system.

SNAP The passing of the football from the center to another offensive player such as the quarterback, punter, or placekick holder. It is a backward pass directed through the legs of the center and signals the start of the play. Also known as centering the ball.

SNAPPER *See* center.

SPEARING A player deliberately tries to injure another player by lunging at him helmet first.

SPECIAL TEAM(S) Players used in kicking situations.

SPIKE To throw the football straight down. Spiking the ball is usually done by players in their opponent's end zone after they have scored a touchdown.

SPIRAL A type of kick or pass in which the football turns on its longer axis as it flies through the air.

SPLIT END (SE) Member of the offensive team who lines up several yards away from the tackle on the side of the line of scrimmage opposite the ball from the tight end. Also called the *wide receiver.*

SPLIT THE UPRIGHTS Term used when referring to the accurate kicking of a field goal or extra point. The kicker kicks the ball so well that it appears as though he "splits" the area between the uprights (goal posts) into two equal parts.

SPOTTING THE BALL The action of the official putting the ball on a certain spot on the ground to start a new play.

SQUIB KICK A kick in which the ball is not kicked far away, rather a kick that is low and short. The strategy behind using a squib kick is to make the ball bounce around, thus making it harder for members of the receiving team to recover and advance.

STRAIGHT ARM A push by the ball carrier with his forearm to prevent his being tackled by an opponent. Also called "stiff arm."

STRIP THE BALL Defensive maneuver in which a tackler tries to get the ball loose from the ball carrier and cause him to fumble. Pulling at the arm of the ball carrier or punching the ball itself as the runner is carrying it are two common ways of stripping the ball.

STRONG SAFETY Defensive player who lines up opposite the offensive team's tight end.

STRONG SIDE The side on the offensive line on which the tight end (TE) lines up.

SUDDEN DEATH If the score is tied at the end of a 60-minute regulation game, the teams continue to play in a 15-minute overtime period. Whichever team scores first wins the game.

SUPER BOWL The final playoff game of the professional football season in which the champion of the American Football Conference (AFC) plays against the champion of the National Football Conference (NFC). The winners of this game are referred to as the Super Bowl Champions or World Champions even though professional football is not played throughout the world.

SWEEP A running play that "sweeps" around one of the ends of the line of scrimmage.

TACKLE The method used by a defensive player to bring a ball carrier to the ground.

TACKLE (T) *See* defensive tackle or offensive tackle.

TAKES THE SNAP Refers to the action of the quarterback in which he receives the ball from the center to begin each play.

TAKING IT TO THE HOUSE *See* all the way.

TEAM AREAS Areas of the football field along the sidelines located between the 35-yard lines where players, coaching staff, and other personnel are found.

TEE A small plastic stand measuring 1" that is used to hold the football in position for the kicker. Tees can be used for kickoffs only. On field goal and extra-point attempts, the ball is held for the placekicker by a teammate holder.

THREE AND OUT The offense runs three plays, does not gain enough yardage for a first down, and must go out of the game; the punting team then comes in to kick the ball to the opponent.

THREE-POINT STANCE A crouched position in which the player has only one hand on the ground.

THROW INTO A CROWD/INTO TRAFFIC Action of the quarterback in which he throws into an area of the field where there are defenders as well as his receivers. A quarterback who frequently throws into a crowd runs the risk of having his passes intercepted by the defense.

THROW IT AWAY Quarterback action in which he throws the ball into an area where there is little chance of a defender intercepting it or his receiver catching it. A quarterback will throw the ball away when he sees that all of his receivers are well-covered, and decides that it would be risky to throw a pass into the well-covered area.

TIGHT END (TE) An offensive player who lines up "tight" next to the tackle on either the right or left hand side on the line of scrimmage. The tight end is part receiver and part offensive lineman. On a passing play he'll go out for a pass; on a running play he'll block.

TIMEOUT Play on the field and the official clock are stopped at the request of either team or the referee for a period of one minute and 50 seconds. The referee crisscrosses his hands above his head to indicate there is a time out on the field. When the referee follows this signal by placing one hand on the top of his cap, it indicates that it is a referee's time out and is not charged to either team.

TOUCHBACK   A touchback occurs when the offensive team puts the ball into the defensive team's end zone on such plays as a kickoff or a punt. The player in possession of the ball remains in his own end zone and goes down on one knee, indicating he will not try to advance the ball beyond the goal line. After a touchback the receiving team becomes the offense and starts the next play on its own 20-yard line.

TOUCHDOWN (TD)   A situation in which the ball, while in possession of a player, is on, above, or behind the opponent's goal line. A touchdown is worth 6 points.

TRAP   A receiver traps the ball when he catches it at the same time as it hits the ground. When the player traps the ball, it is ruled an incomplete pass.

TRENCHES   Refers to the place where the interior line (made up of the left tackle, left guard, center, right guard, and right tackle) meets the defensive linemen.

TRIPPING   A player deliberately extends his foot, causing an opposing player to stumble or fall.

TRY FOR POINT   The play that follows a touchdown in which the team scoring the touchdown can attempt to run, pass or kick the ball over the crossbar of the opponent's goal post. Also called a conversion, extra point, or point after touchdown. If the try for point is successful, one point is scored.

TURNOVER   The offense loses the football to the defense through a fumble or an interception.

TWO MINUTE WARNING   Official's notification to the head coaches of both teams that there are two minutes of playing time remaining in the first and second halves of the game.

UMPIRE (U)   One of the members of the officiating crew. He stands about 5 yards behind the middle defensive lineman and watches the action of the players on the line of scrimmage.

UNCATCHABLE FORWARD PASS   The officials determine that a forward pass was unable to be caught by an intended receiver.

UNDER PRESSURE   Refers to the situation of the quarterback in which he is being pressured by charging members of the defense. When he is under pressure, he is looking to pass the ball quickly to avoid being tackled behind the line of scrimmage for a loss of yards.

UNSPORTSMANLIKE CONDUCT   Any act contrary to the generally understood principles of sportsmanship. The penalty for such an infraction is 15 yards.

UPFIELD   The area beyond the line of scrimmage in the scoring direction of the offense. Also called downfield.

UPRIGHTS   Vertical bars 4' in diameter placed at each end of a horizontal crossbar of a goal post. The uprights rise 30' above the ground; the crossbar and uprights form the goal post.

VETERAN   A professional football player who has been playing for at least one year.

WEAK SAFETY   Member of the defensive backfield who positions himself between the cornerbacks, across from the strong safety and on the opposite side of the line of scrimmage from the offensive team's tight end.

WEAK SIDE   The side of the offensive line away from the tight end.

WIDE RECEIVER (WR)   *See* split end.

WILD CARD   A team that makes the NFL playoffs by having one of the three best records in its conference. Wild card teams are chosen after the six division winners have been identified.

WINNING PERCENTAGE   The percentage of games a team wins out of the total number of games it plays during a certain period of time. For example, in 1994-95, the Pittsburgh Steelers won 12 games out of 16, with a season's winning percentage of .750.

YARDAGE   The unit of measurement in the game of football. Amounts of yardage in certain categories are indicators of performance of a football team.

YARDAGE CHAIN/MARKER Chain measuring 10 yards attached on either end by a 5' high stick that is used to measure distances needed for first downs.

YARDS AFTER CATCH (YAC) The number of yards a receiver gains from the spot on the field where he establishes possession of a passed football to the end of the play.

ZONE An area on the playing field which is defended by certain members of the defensive secondary.

ZONE DEFENSE A type of defensive formation in which each defender is responsible for an area of the field rather than for a specific offensive player.

GLOSSARY OF ABBREVIATIONS & ACRONYMS

AFC	American Football Conference	**OT**	Offensive Tackle
Ast.	Assists	**OT**	Overtime
ATT	Attempts	**PA**	Points Against/Points Allowed
AVG	Average	**PAT**	Point After Touchdown
BJ	Back Judge	**PF**	Points For
Blk.	Blocked	**Pts.**	Points
C	Center	**QB**	Quarterback
COMP.	Completion	**QTR.**	Quarter
CB	Cornerback	**R**	Referee
DB	Defensive Back	**RB**	Running Back
DT	Defensive Tackle	**REC.**	Receptions
FB	Fullback	**Ret. yds.**	Returned Yards
FC	Fair Catch	**Rtng**	Rating
FF	Fumbles Forced	**SAF**	Safety(s)
FG	Field Goal	**Sckd**	Times Sacked
FGA	Field Goals Attempted	**SE**	Split End
FL	Flanker	**SJ**	Side Judge
FR	Fumbles Recovered	**T**	Tackle
FUM	Fumble(s)	**T**	Tie
Fum.Rcvr.	Fumbles Recovered	**TB**	Touchbacks
G	Game	**TD**	Touchdown(s)
GM	Game(s)	**TDM**	Touchdown (s) (Miscellaneous)
GS	Games Started		
HB	Halfback	**TDP**	Touchdowns scored by passing
HL	Head Linesman		
INC.	Incompletion	**TDR**	Touchdowns scored by rushing/running
I.R.	Injured Reserve		
INT	Interception	**TDS**	Touchdowns
L	Losses	**TE**	Tight end
LB	Linebacker	**TK**	Tackles
L/LG	Long	**U**	Umpire
LJ	Line Judge	**W**	Win
MVP	Most Valuable Player	**WR**	Wide Receiver
Net. Diff.	Net Difference	**XP**	Extra Points
NFC	National Football Conference	**XPA**	Extra Points Attempted
		YAC	Yards After Catch
NFL	National Football League	**YDS**	Yards
No.	Number		
OPP	Opponent		

INDEX

245

NOTES

NOTES

NOTES

NOTES